KNIT 2 TOGETHER

Patterns and Stories for Serious Knitting Fun

Mel Clark & Tracey Ullman

PHOTOGRAPHS BY ERIC AXENE

STC Craft | A Melanie Falick Book

STEWART, TABORI & CHANG
New York

To Allan, Mabel, and Johnny, who keep me in stitches.

—Tracey

To India, Pete, and David, for love and understanding.

—Mel

Editor: Melanie Falick
Designer: Anna Christian
Production Manager: Kim Tyner

Library of Congress Cataloging-in-Publication Data:
Ullman, Tracey.
 Knit 2 together : patterns and stories for serious knitting fun / by Tracey Ullman and Mel Clark.
   p. cm.
 "STC Craft/A Melanie Falick Book."
 ISBN 1-58479-534-4
 1. Knitting—Patterns. I. Clark, Mel. II. Title. III. Title: Knit two together.

TT820.U633 2006
746.43'2041—dc22

                    2006001896

Text copyright © 2006 by Tracey Ullman and Mel Clark
Photographs copyright © 2006 by Eric Axene

Published in 2006 by Stewart, Tabori & Chang
An imprint of Harry N. Abrams, Inc.

The text of this book was composed in Balance

Printed and bound in China
10 9 8 7 6 5 4 3 2 1

HNA
harry n. abrams, inc.
a subsidiary of La Martinière Groupe

115 West 18th Street
New York, NY 10011
www.hnabooks.com

Tracey and Mel Take Tea

TRACEY: So, Mel, shall we have a go at writing a book?

MEL: Why not? We always have ideas about things we want to knit, and maybe there are people out there who will want to knit them, too.

TRACEY: I cannot tell you how many people ask me, "How on earth do you do that? I've always wanted to learn." And I tell them, "If I can do it, you can." I encourage them to find a teacher or sign up for lessons at a local yarn store, and not to put it off any longer.

MEL: I want this book to appeal to knitters like you, Tracey, who might just be starting out but quickly realize that they want to learn new skills and take on a challenge. There's no mystery to it. No one need feel intimidated.

TRACEY: It should contain lots of your lovely designs, Mel, and I want to knit a skirt. There are never enough patterns for skirts. And can we please include the dreadlocks I made? I know they're strange but there are others like me out there who want to look like George Clinton of Funkadelic.

MEL: Of course, that's what's great about knitting: You can be unique, and there's always the possibility when you finish it that someone will stop you on the street and ask, "Where did you get that?" And you can smirk and say, "I made it." Which is every knitter's dream.

TRACEY: Exactly. More tea?

MEL: Please.

TRACEY: Shortbread?

MEL: Of course.

TRACEY: I'll put the kettle on and we'll get started. . . .

NEXT
165 PGS

Contents

NICE TO MEET YOU

Tracey's Story

And so it began again . . .

I was taught to do basic knitting by my mother as a child. In, round, through, up; in, round, through, up. "You said threw up, Mummy," I remember replying. The temptation to find the humor in everything was prevalent even then. I liked knitting; it was a nice, comforting, girly thing to do.

Back then my Mum and her friends would get together for weekly "coffee mornings," and one of the ladies I called Auntie Irene would knit at an incredible speed. Her gray metal needles clicked away at 1960s acrylic yarn, making it into bobble hats and matinee jackets. It was also a big decade for the cigarette, and Irene was adept at smoking, gossiping, and knitting, all at the same time. Ash would tumble down her moss-stitch booties as she told the group of Shirley's affair with the golf pro and Pamela's dependence on Valium.

I continued to knit scarves and simple squares for years, never finding out how to increase and decrease. How I longed to follow a pattern, but it seemed as unattainable as learning shorthand or speaking Italian. And heaven forbid I should walk into a wool supply shop in England at the time and ask the stern old spinster behind the counter how to ssk or psso. "Hasn't your mother taught you, young lady?" she would have exclaimed in horror.

I remember at the age of twelve, from economic necessity, unraveling an old wheat-colored cardigan I found in a thrift shop in order to reuse the yarn for a new project. I knitted two big squares for the front and back and two long rectangles for the sleeves and sewed them together. I thought it would make a wonderfully simple, arty-looking sweater. It didn't. It looked like something Fred Flintstone would wear in his cave during a cold snap. And so my inability to ssk, psso, and decrease every 7th row, ending with the WS, continued.

The years went by, and my secret went undiscovered. Then, in the fall of 2003, I took a job in Baltimore, acting in a John Waters movie called *A Dirty Shame* (NC 17. . . beware).

I found myself living next to a wonderful, colonial, English-looking area called Fells Point down by the port. I loved to wander around on my days off with my cavalier King Charles spaniel Frankie, looking into the stores and the old 18th-century red brick houses and talking to the locals.

Opposite my favorite espresso bar was a charming little shop whose windows were filled with a collage of warm autumnal colors, which on closer inspection I realized was yarn. Not the tightly wound, bottle green acrylic type of my youth, but fluffy bundles nestled in rattan baskets with bamboo needles. This yarn looked positively edible! I wanted to go in, but hesitated as I saw a group of rosy-cheeked women sitting around a wooden table. They were talking and creating beautiful shawls, sweaters, and bags. The SSK, PSSO crowd—confident, informed girls who knew their stuff. What would they make of an English scarf enthusiast in her forties? Would they look at me with pity or, even worse, scream with sarcastic laughter?

I was about to jog home, carrying the tubby Frankie, who had ground to a halt, when I saw a sign in the corner of the window that said KNITTING CLASSES. Blimey, I thought. Classes, they let people in on this secret?

Plucking up my courage, I entered the store. A tinkly bell announced my arrival, and a friendly woman named Laraine Guidet, who turned out to be the owner, greeted me. Before I knew it, she was showing me how to knit a bag on bamboo circular needles that I would eventually put into a washing machine and shrink—intentionally! I took a variety of gorgeous yarns home with me and so it began.

Knitting again felt wonderful. It was so calming and timeless. While finishing

the movie, I spent many hours waiting in my trailer making bags, scarves, and eventually a sweater. I had finally unlocked the mystery of following a pattern. I learned that if you can knit with an even tension and are able to add and subtract, you can create anything. I'd broken the barrier and now there was no stopping me.

On my return to Los Angeles, I looked up yarn stores near my home and found Wildfiber. There was a picture of the owner, Mel Clark, on the website, and when I saw it, I had a strange feeling that we would become well acquainted.

I literally rushed over to get new supplies, and was met with the same friendly enthusiasm I had discovered in Baltimore. In Mel's beautiful, light, airy Santa Monica store, there was a communal wooden table, and an even larger selection of the edible yarn. Knitting was enjoying a renaissance and Mel's shop made it obvious why.

My confidence increased in leaps and bounds and six weeks after knitting my felted bag, I was attempting a blackberry stitch jacket designed by Debbie Bliss! I was wielding a cable hook and saying things to my husband like "Sshh, I'm counting increases!"

I must admit, I did throw myself into the knitting bug with a little too much zeal. I stopped reading and cuddling my spaniels. I was putting the needles down at midnight beside my bed, then waking up at six and reaching for them before my first cup of tea. I dreamt of knitting, my hands ached, and I developed a pain in my right shoulder. I have since learnt to walk around a little, stretch, and listen to books on tape.

As I continued to knit I began to notice that, although some great books were available, I preferred the items on display in Mel's shop that she had designed herself. It occurred to me to ask her whether she had thought of publishing her own book and sharing her designs. I have done many things in my career—acting, singing, dancing, dressing up as a Middle Eastern man. I never thought I would want to coproduce a book on knitting, but the subject now intrigued me. So we sat down with a pot of tea and began to make a plan. ⓣ

Mel's Story

I grew up in New Zealand, a land with many more sheep than people.

No wonder, then, that I developed a love of wool at an early age. I remember being about eight years old and my mother sitting me down and teaching me to knit. It immediately became my passion. I loved the puzzle-solving aspect of it, like a crossword or a jigsaw.

Around that time my favorite teacher, Miss McQuilkin, asked the class if anyone had room at home for an abandoned, blind lamb she had brought back from the high country. No sooner had my hand shot up than I found myself being driven home in the back of the teacher's car with "Bunty" on my lap, worried about what my mother would say when she got home from work. Thankfully, my new baby was allowed to stay, and I bottle-fed her in the kitchen until "he" sprouted horns and my parents relegated him to the backyard, where he did a nice job fertilizing the lawn.

I continued to knit all the way through my teens, spending my lunch breaks during high school sitting outside on the tennis courts, working on my latest project while tanning my legs. None of my friends knitted, but that didn't stop me. I was obsessed! A good source of patterns at the time was an English magazine called *Woman's Weekly*. I remember knitting a very complicated Aran skirt and sweater from it. It took me ages, and when I finished it, I realized that it didn't look as good on me as it did on the famous model, Jean Shrimpton. So I sold the sweater to my best friend's mother and turned the skirt into a pillow. Knitting that suit was a milestone for me. I had never knitted cables before, so it taught me that I could tackle any knitting pattern as long as I was willing to read the instructions and learn the techniques.

In the early 1980s, after I had married and had my son, my husband's job took us away from New Zealand to different countries for long periods of time. I found myself in places like London, Tahiti, and North Carolina, always looking for a yarn shop. While I was living in London I discovered Patricia Roberts's innovative knitting shop in Covent Garden, one of the most exciting stores I had ever been in—light and airy and jam-packed with color—and I thought her designs were fantastic. My favorite was a traditional argyle pattern in hot-colored silks and angoras, embellished with cables. Being around those amazing yarns inspired me to go home and start creating my own designs. My first efforts were little multicolored cardigans for my two-year-old son, knitted during his afternoon naps.

Eventually, my family and I settled in California, and I decided to start a cottage industry designing sweaters that were handknitted in New Zealand. My first designs proved to be popular, and I began selling them to boutiques across the United States. At one point I had more than a hundred knitters following my complicated graphs and doing exquisite work—women of all ages, in towns and on remote farms, and one man who was a widower with six children and needed the extra income. I also supplied LL Bean with exclusive sweater designs during the 1990s.

I wasn't knitting much during this time, but I was brought back to it when a costume designer commissioned me to make a vest for the movie *Fear and Loathing in Las Vegas*. Although she had used my designs before in other movies, I had never actually knitted them myself. I sat and knitted for three days straight to make a striped, ribbed biker vest, and this experience reminded me how much I loved to knit and how much I missed the company of other knitters.

To rectify the situation, I decided to teach knitting classes in my home studio and at a local fiber arts store called Wildfiber. Soon after starting at Wildfiber I found out the owner wanted to sell the business and I decided to buy it and turn it exclusively into a yarn shop, which was scary to me since the knitting resurgence had not yet begun. But I felt like I had to follow my dream. In the beginning I wondered if there would be enough people in sunny southern California who would want to make sweaters, but I quickly realized that a lot of people do want to make sweaters here and also that yarns these days are so varied you can knit anything you want, from sweaters to handbags, curtains, and pillows. Even old-fashioned doilies are fun.

For me, it's exciting that so many people have now discovered this wonderful, comforting craft that I have loved my whole life. I continue to be a passionate knitter, and designing new patterns is always a thrill. I never know if an idea is going to work out just the way I imagined it, but it's always fun, and the excitement of finishing a new project and realizing that I love it can still keep me awake at night.

When I met Tracey I realized that she wanted to make things that weren't available in books. She had very quickly become an intrepid knitter, my favorite kind, and it was hard to keep up with her.

So when she asked me if I wanted to sit down with a pot of tea and talk about doing a book of our own, I agreed. It was time. Ⓜ

Golden Rules for Knitting

MEL'S GOLDEN RULES

● Take a risk. It's not dangerous.

● It's supposed to be fun, so don't let it make you crazy.

● Be prepared to make mistakes and learn from them.

TRACEY'S GOLDEN RULES

● Tell anyone who says knitting makes you look grannyish to get lost.

● In my opinion, holiday sweaters shouldn't be worn at ANY time of year.

● If you're on a plane and get horribly stuck on a pattern, you can always ask the captain to make the announcement, "Is there a knitter on board?"

WHAT WE LIKE TO KNIT
(Mel's Patterns)

BABY BASEBALL TEE WITH MITTENS

This raglan pullover is one of the first projects I teach in my beginner classes. The simple inset center pocket delights everyone and can be used to hold the matching mittens. For a great parent-child set, make this sweater for your baby and then a Santa Cruz Hoodie (see page 88) in a coordinating color for yourself. **Ⓜ TRACEY WARNS:** *Do this before your kids turn into teenagers and find you an enormous embarrassment.*

SIZES
To fit Infant (3 months)

FINISHED MEASUREMENTS
18¹/₂" (47 cm) chest

YARN
Rowan Wool Cotton (50% merino wool / 50% cotton; 123 yards (112 meters) / 50 grams): 2 balls #901 citron (A), 1 ball #941 clear (B)

NEEDLES
One pair straight needles size US 5 (3.75 mm)

One pair straight needles size US 3 (3.25 mm)

One pair double-pointed needles (dpn) size US 2 (3 mm) for Mittens

Change needle size if necessary to obtain correct gauge

NOTIONS
Row markers; stitch holders; stitch markers; two ³/₈" buttons

GAUGE
22 sts and 31 rows = 4" (10 cm) in Stockinette st (St st) using largest needles

BACK

Using size US 3 needles and A, cast on 51 sts; begin Garter st. Work even for 4 rows.

Change to larger needles.

Row 1 (WS): K3, purl to last 3 sts, k3.

Row 2: Knit.

Repeat Rows 1-2 twice. Repeat Row 1. Place row marker at beginning and end of row for side seams.

(RS) Change to St st, beginning with a knit row, and work even until piece measures 7" from the beginning, ending with a WS row.

Shape Raglan Armhole: (RS) Bind off 2 sts at beginning of next 2 rows.

Decrease 1 st each side every other row 14 times, as follows: K1, ssk, work to last 3 sts, k2tog, k1—19 sts remain.

(WS) Change to size US 3 needles and Garter st. Work even for 3 rows.

Bind off all sts loosely knitwise.

POCKET LINING

Using larger needle and B, cast on 17 sts. (RS) Work even in St st, beginning with a knit row, for 21 rows.

Break yarn, leaving a 20" tail. Place stitches on a holder for Pocket.

FRONT

Work as for Back until piece measures 4" from the beginning, ending with a RS row.

POCKET

Setup Row 1: (WS) P17, k17, p17.

Row 2: Knit.

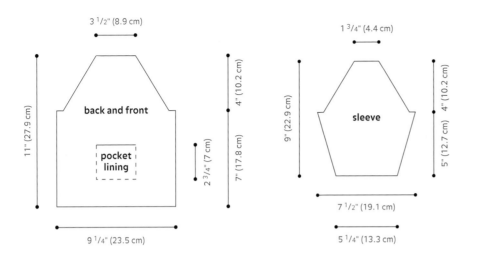

back and front
3 1/2" (8.9 cm)
11" (27.9 cm)
pocket lining
2 3/4" (7 cm)
4" (10.2 cm)
7" (17.8 cm)
9 1/4" (23.5 cm)

sleeve
1 3/4" (4.4 cm)
9" (22.9 cm)
4" (10.2 cm)
5" (12.7 cm)
7 1/2" (19.1 cm)
5 1/4" (13.3 cm)

Row 3: Repeat Row 1.

Row 4: K17, bind off center 17 sts, knit to end.

Row 5: P17, slip sts from Pocket Lining holder onto left-hand needle with WS of Pocket Lining facing, purl to end.

Continue in St st, beginning with a knit row, until piece measures 7" from the beginning, ending with a WS row. Complete as for Back.

SLEEVES (make 2)
Using size US 3 needles and B, cast on 29 sts; begin Garter st. Work even for 4 rows.

(WS) Change to larger needles and St st, beginning with a purl row. Work even for 3 rows.

Shape Sleeve: (RS) Increase 1 st each side this row, then every 4 rows 5 times—41 sts. Work even until piece measures 5" from the beginning, ending with a WS row.

Shape Raglan: (RS) Bind off 2 sts at beginning of next 2 rows—37 sts remain.

Decrease 1 st each side every other row 14 times, as follows: K1, ssk, work to last 3 sts, k2tog, k1—9 sts remain.

(WS) Change to size US 3 needles and Garter st. Work even for 3 rows. Bind off all sts knitwise.

FINISHING
Sew left raglan seams. Sew right back raglan seam.

Buttonhole Placket: RS of Front facing, using size US 3 needles and B, pick up and knit 23 sts from neck to underarm, stopping before bound-off sts at underarm.

Make Buttonholes: (WS) K11, yo, k2tog, k6, yo, k2tog, k2.

Knit 2 rows. Bind off all sts knitwise.

Button Placket: RS of right Sleeve facing, using size US 3 needles and B, pick up and knit 23 sts from beginning of raglan shaping to neck.

Knit 1 row. Bind off all sts knitwise.

Sew Sleeve seams. Sew underarm seams. Sew side seams from underarm to row markers, leaving last 11 rows open for side slit.

Stitch end of Buttonhole Placket to Sleeve at armhole. Sew buttons opposite buttonholes.

Block Pocket Lining. Pin to WS of Front. Using B, sew Lining to Front, being careful not to let sts show on RS.

Use metal needles for an itch that's hard to reach.

MITTENS (make 2)

Using size US 3 needles and A, cast on 22 sts; begin Garter st. Work even for 4 rows.

(WS) Change to largest needles and St st, beginning with a purl row. Work even for 3 rows.

Eyelet Row (RS): K1, *yo, k2tog, k1; repeat from * to end.

Work even in St st for 3 rows, beginning with a purl row.

THUMB

Row 1 (RS): K10, place marker (pm), [kfb] twice, pm, k10—24 sts.

Rows 2, 4, and 6: Purl.

Row 3: K10, slip marker (sm), kfb, k2, kfb, sm, k10—26 sts.

Row 5: K10, sm, kfb, k4, kfb, sm, k10—28 sts.

Row 7: K10, sm, kfb, k6, kfb, sm, k10—30 sts.

Row 8: P10, sm, p10, place remaining 10 sts on a holder for Fingers, turn.

Row 9: K10, place remaining 10 sts on a holder for Fingers.

Next Row (WS): Working on center 10 sts only, work even in St st for 3 rows, beginning with a purl row.

Next Row (RS): *K2tog; repeat from * to end—5 sts remain.

Break yarn and thread through remaining sts. Pull tight and fasten off. Sew Thumb seam.

FINGERS

WS facing, rejoin yarn to base of Thumb; pick up and purl 2 sts from base of Thumb, purl across 10 sts from first holder—12 sts.

(RS) K12, knit across 10 sts from second holder—22 sts.

Work in St st for 5 rows, beginning with a purl row.

Shape Top: (RS) Skp, k7, k2tog, ssk, k7, k2tog—18 sts remain. Purl 1 row.

(RS) Skp, k5, k2tog, ssk, k5, k2tog—14 sts remain. Purl 1 row.

(RS) Skp, k3, k2tog, ssk, k3, k2tog—10 sts remain.

Break yarn, leaving a 10" tail.

Divide sts evenly between 2 dpn (5 sts each). Graft sts together using Kitchener st (see page 164).

Sew side seams. Weave in ends.

TIES

Using dpn, cast on 2 sts and work I-cord (see page 164) 5" long; fasten off.

Thread I-cord through eyelets and tie.

You Can Have Enough Scarves

A scarf is easy to knit and probably one of the first things you will attempt. Great. Then move on. Challenge yourself. Not progressing from knitting scarves is like riding a bike with training wheels forever, or only allowing yourself to listen to one Beatles song.

Remember, I was a scarf knitter for forty years and now I have become, as Mel puts it, "intrepid." Oh, the time I wasted. Increasing and decreasing are such easy skills to learn, and once you do, you can tackle most anything.

I knitted booties and a jacket for a friend's baby shower recently. The gasps of admiration I got from the other guests were well worth the effort. And seeing the baby two months later, lying on a blanket with his chubby clenched fists poking out of the sleeves, was incredible. I was not so thrilled by the blob of regurgitated milk on the collar, but I'm sure he didn't mean to disrespect my handiwork.

So, knit a sweater, socks, something with buttonholes. Don't set yourself a time limit and be prepared to unravel mistakes . . . and I promise you will feel an enormous sense of achievement and pride when someone exclaims, "You knitted that?!" 🅣

FIRST HAT

This easy hat is knit in the round with alternate bands of knit and purl stitches for texture. If you're a beginner, don't be daunted by the double-pointed needles used for the decreases at the crown. They're simple to use and you'll be pleased with the seamless results. The flower is fun to make and transforms the hat from a beanie to a stylish cloche. **Ⓜ** TRACEY SAYS: *I repeat, do not be daunted by double-pointed needles. Quite simply, you're spacing the stitches out onto four needles instead of two. It's a bit fiddly holding them all at first, but it makes you look ever so clever.*

SIZES
Small (Medium)

FINISHED MEASUREMENTS
18 (19 1/2)" (45.7 (49.5) cm) circumference

YARN
Rio de la Plata Santa Maria Merino Collection (100% wool; 164 yards (150 meters) / 99 grams): *One-Color Hat and Flower:* 1 hank PL 95 sky blue; *Two-Color Hat:* 1 hank each PL 65 rabbit (A) and PL 8 red brick (B)

NEEDLES
One 16" (40 cm) circular (circ) needle size US 9 (5.5 mm)

One set 8" double-pointed needles (dpn) size US 9 (5.5 mm)

One pair straight needles size US 9 (5.5 mm)

Change needle size if necessary to obtain correct gauge.

NOTIONS
Stitch marker; 1 1/2" button

GAUGE
16 sts and 24 rows = 4" (10 cm) in Stockinette st (St st)

ONE-COLOR HAT

Using circ needle, cast on 72 (78) sts. Join for working in the rnd, being careful not to twist sts; place marker (pm) for beginning of rnd.

Knit 4 rnds. Purl for 3". Knit for 2".

Purl 5 rnds. Knit 5 rnds. Purl 5 rnds.

Shape Hat: Change to dpn.

Rnd 1: *K4, k2tog; repeat from * to end of rnd—60 (65) sts remain.

Rnd 2 and all even-numbered rnds: Knit.

Rnd 3: *K3, k2tog; repeat from * to end of rnd—48 (52) sts remain.

Rnd 5: *K2, K2tog; repeat from * to end of rnd—36 (39) sts remain.

Rnd 7: *K1, k2tog; repeat from * to end of rnd—24 (26) sts remain.

Rnd 9: *K2tog; repeat from * to end of rnd—12 (13) sts remain.

Knit 1 rnd.

Break yarn, leaving a 12" tail, thread through remaining sts and pull tight. Weave in ends.

FLOWER PETAL (make 5)
Using straight needles, cast on 4 sts. Knit 1 row.

*Work Increase Row as follows: Kfb, knit to last st, kfb—6 sts.

Knit 1 row. Repeat from * once—8 sts.

Break yarn and leave on needle.

Join Petals: With all 5 Petals on one needle, knit across 8 sts of each Petal—40 sts.

Shape Flower: * K1, k2tog, k2, k2tog, k1; repeat from * to end—30 sts remain. Purl 1 row.

*K1, [k2tog] twice, k1; repeat from * to end—20 sts remain.

*P2tog; repeat from * to end—10 sts remain.

Thread yarn through remaining sts, pull tight and fasten off.

Sew seam between first and last Petal.

Sew Flower to Hat with button in center of Flower. Weave in ends.

TWO-COLOR HAT

Using circ needle and A, cast on 72 (78) sts. Join for working in the rnd, being careful not to twist sts; place marker (pm) for beginning of rnd. Knit 4 rnds. Purl for 3".

Change to B and knit for 2".

Change to A and knit 1 rnd. Purl 5 rnds.

Change to B and knit 5 rnds.

Change to A and knit 1 rnd. Purl 5 rnds.

Shape Hat: Change to dpn and B. Complete as for One-Color Hat.

Typical Reactions When People See Us Knitting

TRACEY
You?! Why?

My Granny did that.

Are you starting menopause?

Knit me a conservatory for the back of my house. (my witty friend Mandy in England)

MEL
You know what I'd love you to knit for me?

Have you decided what you'd like for dinner, Ma'am. Ooh, what are you knitting?

Honk, honk! The light's green, Lady.

Talk Around the Table

There is a large wooden table at Wildfiber that brings people together to knit. I rarely do anything group-oriented—as I live in Los Angeles, where if you say you have a "class," people think it's either power Pilates, or you're in a twelve-step program. But I occasionally sit around this table, drink tea, and strike up a conversation with people I have never met before.

There's something about not being able to look someone directly in the eye for fear of dropping a stitch that seems to make you lose your inhibitions. Intimate subjects can be intensely debated as you yo, k1, turn. Plastic surgery is a big one—who has had it, who wants it, and who would never have it. Sex is also high on the agenda, and I have heard more than one new knitter compare an orgasm to the completion of a poncho and then decide that the poncho was more satisfying.

Politics, as in most social situations, is to be avoided at the table. There's nothing worse than thinking you have a general consensus on an issue, only to be startled when the shy woman who knits in pastels makes a row-dropping comment on foreign policy, something that sets her a little to the right of Genghis Khan.

You can tell when a group of knitters is shocked because the clicking stops, and some of us even look up. I usually dive in with a diversionary strategy in these situations, like asking, "Do you know if needles are allowed on international flights now?" Or, if that fails, I fall back on the classic female ice-breaker: "Who do you think is better looking, Brad Pitt or George Clooney?"

But, generally, the conversations that spring forth at the table are warm and meditative. When you're there, you feel like you are a part of a timeless chain of female bonding. Knitting is not a competitive sport; there is no race to the finish. The very rhythmic nature of the task doesn't seem to allow it. So we all sit back, turn off our bloody cell phones, and let the yarn slide through our fingers. Very soon we may be debating the meaning of life—and whether it involves nuclear energy, laser resurfacing, or female Viagra. ⓣ

GROWNUP BONNET

This scarf is one of the most popular projects at Wildfiber. I decided it would be fun and convenient to add a romantic hood and have two in one. First you knit the scarf, achieving the flared, fluted edge by beginning with a knit 3, purl 3 rib, then shifting into a knit 2, purl 2 rib. Next, you pick up stitches for the bonnet and knit it from back to front. Of course, you could stop with the scarf and skip the bonnet if you prefer. **M** TRACEY ASKS: *Why should bonnets remain forever exclusive to babies and shepherdesses?*

SIZES
One size

FINISHED MEASUREMENTS
Bonnet: 22" (55.9 cm) circumference; Scarf: 4" (10.2 cm) wide x 55" (139.7 cm) long, slightly stretched

YARN
Blue Sky Alpaca Worsted (50% alpaca / 50% wool; 100 yards (91.4 meters) / 100 grams): 4 hanks #2010 rusty orange

NEEDLES
One 24" (60 cm) circular (circ) needle size US 10 (6 mm)

One 24" (60 cm) circular needle size US 9 (5.5 mm)

Change needle size if necessary to obtain correct gauge.

NOTIONS
Stitch markers

GAUGE
15 sts and 20 rows = 4" (10 cm) in Stockinette st (St st) using larger needle

NOTES
The Bonnet is meant to be roomy. See instructions for making a smaller Bonnet or longer Scarf, if desired. Be sure to purchase additional yarn if you plan to make a longer scarf.

SCARF

Using smaller needles, cast on 41 sts; begin 3x3 Rib as follows:

Row 1 (RS): P1, *k3, p3; repeat from * to last 4 sts, k3, p1.

Row 2: K1, *p3, k3; repeat from * to last 4 sts, p3, k1.

Repeat Rows 1 and 2 six times.

Shape Scarf: (RS) Change to 2x2 Rib as follows:

Row 1: P1, *k1, k2tog, p3; repeat from * to last 4 sts, k1, k2tog, p1—34 sts remain.

Row 2: K1, *p2, k1, k2tog; repeat from * to last 3 sts, p2, k1—28 sts remain.

Row 3: P1, *k2, p2; repeat from * to last 3 sts, k2, p1.

Row 4: K1, *p2, k2; repeat from * to last 3 sts, p2, k1.

Repeat Rows 3 and 4 until Scarf measures 50" or desired length less 5", ending with a WS row.

(RS) Change to 3x3 Rib as follows:

Row 1: P1, *k1, m1, k1, p2; repeat from * to last 3 sts, k1, m1, k1, p1—35 sts.

Row 2: K1, *p3, k1, m1, k1; repeat from * to last 4 sts, p3, k1—41 sts.

Row 3: P1, *k3, p3; repeat from * to last 4 sts, k3, p1.

Row 4: K1, *p3, k3; repeat from * to last 4 sts, p3, k1.

Repeat Rows 3 and 4 six times.

Bind off all sts in Rib. Weave in all ends.

Tracey Woolman

It was pointed out to me by our editor for this book that the word *Ull* means wool in Norwegian. So my last name—Ullman—literally translated, is Woolman. This suggests that my ancestors may have been shepherds, spinners, or wool merchants.

When I think about this, I imagine my family lugging great bales of wool to icy Oslo marketplaces in the Middle Ages. Maybe the actress Liv Ullman is a long lost cousin of mine and her branch of the Ullmans had the stall next to ours. Good thing we girls weren't around back then, because I don't think we would have been allowed to pursue anything like our 21st-century occupations, as Ingmar Bergman's muse and a cross-dressing comedienne. We probably would have been shearing sheep beside a fjord and spinning yarn during those long winter months.

Tracey Woolman—this discovery seems prophetic to me, and maybe explains my newfound love for everything related to yarn. After all, it's in my blood. **T**

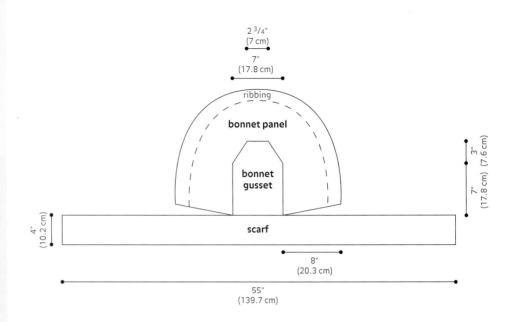

BONNET

Mark center of long side of Scarf. Place two markers 3 1/2" to either side of center marker; remove center marker. Using smaller needle, pick up and knit 26 sts between markers for Bonnet Gusset.

(WS) Work even in St st for 5 rows, beginning with a purl row. Change to larger needle and work even until Gusset measures 7" from the beginning, ending with a WS row.

Shape Gusset:

Row 1 (RS): Skp, knit to last 2sts, k2tog—24 sts remain.

Row 2: Purl.

Rows 3-6: Repeat Rows 1 and 2 twice—20 sts remain after Row 5.

Row 7: Skp, knit to last 2 sts, k2tog—18 sts remain.

Row 8: Spp, purl to last 2 sts, p2tog—16 sts remain.

Rows 9-10: Repeat Rows 7 and 8—12 sts remain after Row 10.

Row 11: Repeat Row 7—10 sts remain.

Bind off all sts. Break yarn, leaving a 12" tail.

Bonnet Panel: RS facing, using larger needle and beginning at right base of Gusset near Scarf edge, pick up and knit 86 sts around Gusset as follows: 38 sts along right side, 10 sts across top, 38 sts along left side.

(WS) Work even in St st for 6", beginning with a purl row. *NOTE: Work even for*

4" for 18" circumference or 5" for 20" circumference.

Ribbed Edging: (RS) Change to smaller needle and 2x2 Rib as follows:

Row 1 (RS): *K2, p2; repeat from * to last 2 sts, k2.

Row 2: *P2, k2; repeat from * to last 2 sts, p2.

Rows 3-4: Repeat Rows 1 and 2.

Row 5: Repeat Row 1.

Row 6: Change to 3x3 Rib as follows: *P2, k1, m1, k1; repeat from * to last 2 sts, p2—107 sts.

Row 7: K2, p3, *k1, m1, k1, p3; repeat from * to last 2 sts, k2—127 sts.

Row 8: P2, k3, *p3, k3; repeat from * to last 2 sts, p2.

Row 9: K2, p3, *k3, p3; repeat from * to last 2 sts, k2.

Row 10: Repeat Row 8.

Bind off all sts in Rib, leaving a long tail.

FINISHING

Measure 7 1/2" to either side of Gusset on Scarf edge; pm. Thread tail through edge sts of Bonnet from Ribbed Edging to Gusset. Gather slightly to a width of 7 1/2" [5 1/2" for 18" circumference; 6 1/2" for 20" circumference]; pin to edge of Scarf, between Gusset and marker, and sew in place. Repeat with other side of Bonnet. Weave in ends.

ROWENA CARDIGAN

This feminine cardigan provides an opportunity to show off your favorite ribbons. They are threaded though the neck and may also be threaded through the cuffs and hem, and may be changed at your whim. The wide raglan neckline gives a relaxed, romantic look that works well with jeans, over a pretty dress, or with a skirt for an evening out. **M**

SIZES
To fit 32 (34, 36, 38, 40)" (81.3 (86.4, 91.4, 96.5, 101.6) cm) bust

Shown in size 34" (86.4 cm)

FINISHED MEASUREMENTS
32 1/2 (34, 36, 38, 40)" 82.6 (86.4, 91.4, 96.5, 101.6) cm bust

YARN
Lana Gatto Feeling (70% wool / 20% silk / 10% cashmere; 153 yards (140 meters) / 50 grams): 10 (10, 11, 11, 11) balls #12482

NEEDLES
One pair straight needles size US 4 (3.5 mm)

One pair straight needles size US 5 (3.75 mm)

One 29" circular (circ) needle size US 4 (3.5 mm)

Change needle size if necessary to obtain correct gauge.

NOTIONS
Stitch holder; 2 yards 1" Hannah Silk Ribbon in terrazzo for neck (plus an additional 1 1/2 yards for sleeves and 2 1/2 yards for hem, if desired); 5 (5, 5, 5, 6) 3/4" buttons

GAUGE
25 sts and 32 rows = 4" (10 cm) in Stockinette stitch (St st) using larger needles

NOTES
When stitching turned hems on the WS, be careful to catch the part of the st that is closest to the WS surface. This will make the hemline less visible on the RS.

BACK

Using smaller needles, cast on 101 (107, 113, 119, 125) sts. Work even in St st for 11 rows, beginning with a knit row.

Next Row (WS): Knit (fold line).

Work Ruching: (RS) *Kfb; repeat from * to end—202 (214, 226, 238, 250) sts.

(WS) Work even in St st for 11 rows, beginning with a purl row.

Next Row (RS): *K2tog; repeat from * to end—101 (107, 113, 119, 125) sts remain.

Knit 1 row.

(RS) Change to larger needles. Work even in St st, beginning with a knit row, until piece measures 14 (14, 15, 15, 15)" from fold line.

Shape Raglan Armholes: (RS) Bind off 3 sts at beginning of next 2 rows—95 (101, 107, 113, 119) sts remain.

(RS) Decrease 1 st each side every other row 21 (23, 24, 26, 28) times, as follows: Skp, work to last 2 sts, k2tog—53 (55, 59, 61, 63) sts remain.

Purl 1 row.

Shape Neck: (RS) Right Side: Skp, k5, place remaining 46 (48, 52, 54, 56) sts on holder for left side, turn work—6 sts remain.

Next Row (WS): Bind off 1 st, work to end—5 sts remain.

Skp, k1, k2tog—3 sts remain. Purl 1 row.

Sk2p—1 st remains. Fasten off.

(RS) Left Side: Rejoin yarn to sts on holder, bind off 39 (41, 45, 47, 49) sts for neck, work to last 2 sts, k2tog—6 sts remain.

Next Row (WS): Work to last 2 sts, p2tog—5 sts remain.

Skp, k1, k2tog—3 sts remain.

Sp2p—1 st remains. Fasten off.

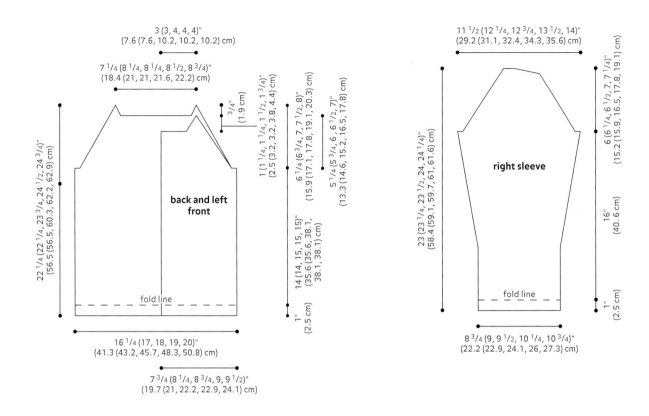

back and left front

3 (3, 4, 4, 4)"
(7.6 (7.6, 10.2, 10.2, 10.2) cm)

7 1/4 (8 1/4, 8 1/4, 8 1/2, 8 3/4)"
(18.4 (21, 21, 21.6, 22.2) cm)

3/4"
(1.9 cm)

1 (1 1/4, 1 1/4, 1 1/2, 1 3/4)"
(2.5 (3.2, 3.2, 3.8, 4.4) cm)

6 1/4 (6 3/4, 7, 7 1/2, 8)"
(15.9 (17.1, 17.8, 19.1, 20.3) cm)

5 1/4 (5 3/4, 6, 6 1/2, 7)"
(13.3 (14.6, 15.2, 16.5, 17.8) cm)

22 1/4 (22 1/4, 23 3/4, 24 1/2, 24 3/4)"
(56.5 (56.5, 60.3, 62.2, 62.9) cm)

14 (14, 15, 15, 15)"
(35.6 (35.6, 38.1, 38.1, 38.1) cm)

1"
(2.5 cm)

fold line

16 1/4 (17, 18, 19, 20)"
(41.3 (43.2, 45.7, 48.3, 50.8) cm)

7 3/4 (8 1/4, 8 3/4, 9, 9 1/2)"
(19.7 (21, 22.2, 22.9, 24.1) cm)

right sleeve

11 1/2 (12 1/4, 12 3/4, 13 1/2, 14)"
(29.2 (31.1, 32.4, 34.3, 35.6) cm)

6 (6 1/4, 6 1/2, 7, 7 1/4)"
(15.2 (15.9, 16.5, 17.8, 19.1) cm)

23 (23 1/4, 23 1/2, 24, 24 1/4)"
(58.4 (59.1, 59.7, 61, 61.6) cm)

16"
(40.6 cm)

fold line

1"
(2.5 cm)

8 3/4 (9, 9 1/2, 10 1/4, 10 3/4)"
(22.2 (22.9, 24.1, 26, 27.3) cm)

LEFT FRONT

Using smaller needles, cast on 48 (51, 54, 57, 60) sts. Work as for Back to beginning of armhole shaping, ending with a WS row.

Shape Raglan Armhole: (RS) Bind off 3 sts, work to end—45 (48, 51, 54, 57) sts remain.

Decrease Row 1 (WS): Work to last 2 sts, p2tog—44 (47, 50, 53, 56) sts remain.

Decrease Row 2: Skp, work to end—43 (46, 49, 52, 55) sts remain.

Repeat Decrease Rows 1 and 2 once—41 (44, 47, 50, 53) sts remain. Work even for 1 row.

(RS) Work Decrease Row 2 this row, then every other row 12 (13, 14, 15, 16) times—28 (30, 32, 34, 36) sts remain.

Shape Neck: (WS) Bind off 7 sts at neck edge twice and, AT THE SAME TIME, decrease 1 st at armhole edge every RS row as established twice—12 (14, 16, 18, 20) sts remain.

Decrease Row 1: (WS) Spp, work to end—11 (13, 15, 17, 19) sts remain.

Decrease Row 2: Skp, work to last 2 sts, k2tog—9 (11, 13, 15, 17) sts remain.

(WS) Repeat Decrease Rows 1 and 2 2 (3, 3, 4, 5) times—3 (2, 4, 3, 2) sts remain.

Size 36 Only: Repeat Decrease Row 1 once—3 sts remain.

All Sizes: Sp2p (spp, sk2p, sp2p, spp). Fasten off.

RIGHT FRONT

Work as for Left Front to beginning of armhole shaping, ending with a RS row.

Shape Raglan Armhole: (WS) Bind off 3 sts, work to end—45 (48, 51, 54, 57) sts remain.

Decrease Row 1 (RS): Work to last 2 sts, k2tog—44 (47, 50, 53, 56) sts remain.

When counting stitches, make sure you get the same count twice.

Decrease Row 2: Spp, work to end—43 (46, 49, 52, 55) sts remain.

Repeat Decrease Rows 1 and 2 once—41 (44, 47, 50, 53) sts remain.

(RS) Work Decrease Row 1 this row, then every other row 12 (13, 14, 15, 16) times, ending with a WS row—28 (30, 32, 34, 36) sts remain.

Shape Neck: (RS) Bind off 7 sts at neck edge twice and, AT THE SAME TIME, decrease 1 st at armhole edge every RS row as established twice, ending with a WS row—12 (14, 16, 18, 20) sts remain.

Decrease Row 1 (RS): Skp, work to last 2 sts, k2tog—10 (12, 14, 16, 18) sts remain.

Decrease Row 2: Work to last 2 sts, p2tog—9 (11, 13, 15, 17) sts remain.

(RS) Repeat Decrease Rows 1 and 2 2 (3, 3, 4, 5) times—3 (2, 4, 3, 2) sts remain.

Size 36 Only: Repeat Decrease Row 1 once—2 sts remain.

All Sizes: Sk2p (skp, spp, sk2p, skp).

Fasten off.

RIGHT SLEEVE

Using smaller needles, cast on 54 (56, 60, 64, 68) sts. Work as for Back until Ruching decreases are complete. Knit 1 row.

(RS) Change to larger needles and St st, beginning with a knit row. Work even for 18 rows.

Shape Sleeve (RS): Increase 1 st each side this row, then every 8 (8, 6, 6, 6) rows 8 (9, 9, 9, 9) times—72 (76, 80, 84, 88) sts.

Work even until piece measures 16" or to desired length from fold line, ending with a WS row.

Shape Raglan: (RS) BO 3 sts at beginning of next 2 rows—66 (70, 74, 78, 82) sts remain.

Decrease Row 1 (RS): Skp, work to last 2 sts, k2tog—64 (68, 72, 76, 80) sts remain.

Decrease Row 2 (WS): Work to last 2 sts, p2tog—63 (67, 71, 75, 79) sts remain.

Repeat Decrease Rows 1 and 2 once—60 (64, 68, 72, 76) sts remain.

Repeat Decrease Row 1 this row, then every other row 18 (19, 20, 22, 23) times—

22 (24, 26, 26, 28) sts remain. Work even for 1 row.

Next Row (RS): Bind off 7 sts, work to last 2 sts, k2tog—14 (16, 18, 18, 20) sts remain.

Spp, work to end—13 (15, 17, 17, 19) sts remain.

Repeat last 2 rows once—4 (6, 8, 8, 10) sts remain.

Bind off all sts.

LEFT SLEEVE

Work as for Right Sleeve to beginning of Raglan Shaping, ending with a RS row.

Shape Raglan: (WS) Bind off 3 sts at beginning of next 2 rows—66 (70, 74, 78, 82) sts remain.

Decrease Row 1 (WS): Spp, work to end—65 (69, 73, 77, 81) sts remain.

Decrease Row 2 (RS): Skp, work to last 2 sts, k2tog—63 (67, 71, 75, 79) sts remain.

Repeat Decrease Rows 1 and 2 once—60 (64, 68, 72, 76) sts remain. Work even for 1 row.

Repeat Decrease Row 2 this row, then every other row 18 (19, 20, 22, 23) times—22 (24, 26, 26, 28) sts remain.

Next row (WS): Bind off 7 sts, work to last 2 sts, p2tog—14 (16, 18, 18, 20) sts remain.

Skp, work to end—13 (15, 17, 17, 19) sts remain.

Repeat last 2 rows once—4 (6, 8, 8, 10) sts remain.

Bind off all sts.

FINISHING

Sew Sleeves to Front and Back along raglan edges, being careful to match right Sleeve with right Front, and left Sleeve with left Front.

Neckband: RS facing, using circ needle, beginning at right Front, pick up and knit 27 (29, 32, 34, 35) sts along right Front neck edge, 19 (20, 21, 22, 23) sts across right Sleeve, 52 (55, 59, 62, 64) sts across Back neck edge, 19 (20, 21, 22, 23) sts across left Sleeve, 27 (29, 32, 34, 35) sts along left Front neck edge—144 (153, 165, 174, 180) sts. Knit 1 row.

Next Row (RS): K1, *kfb; repeat from * to last st, k1—286 (304, 328, 346, 358) sts. Work even in St st for 11 rows.

Next Row (RS): K1, *k2tog; repeat from * to last st, k1—144 (153, 165, 174, 180) sts remain.

Knit 1 row (fold line). Work even in St st for for 8 rows.

Next Row (RS): K3, *kfb, k2; repeat from * to end—191 (203, 219, 231, 239) sts. Purl 1 row. Knit 1 row.

Bind off all sts.

Fold Neckband to WS at fold line; stitch to pick-up row. Leave ends open to thread ribbon through.

Buttonhole Band: RS facing, using smaller needles and beginning at lower edge of right Front, pick up and knit 9 sts along top layer of Ruching, 90 (92, 98, 99, 103) sts along Front edge to beginning of Neckband, and 9 sts along top layer of Neckband (being careful not to close Neckband opening)—108 (110, 116, 117, 121) sts. Begin Garter st. Work even for 1 row.

(RS) Bind off 9 sts at beginning of next 2 rows—90 (92, 98, 99, 103) sts remain.

Make Buttonholes: (RS) K4 (3, 4, 5, 3), *bind off next 2 sts, k17 (18, 19, 19, 16); repeat from * 3 (3, 3, 3, 4) times, bind off 2 sts, k3 (2, 3, 3, 2).

Next Row (RS): Knit, casting on 2 sts over bound-off sts of previous row.

Work even in Garter st for 4 rows. Bind off all sts loosely.

Button Band: Work as for Buttonhole Band, beginning at upper edge of left Front and omitting buttonholes.

Sew side and Sleeve seams. Fold bottom edge of Sleeve to WS at fold line; stitch to WS, leaving an opening in the ruched edging to thread ribbon through (optional). Fold bottom edge of Back and Fronts to WS at fold line; stitch to WS. Split yarn and use a single strand to sew buttons opposite buttonholes. Thread ribbon through Neckband.

Start a new **ball** of yarn at the **beginning** of a row.

LINEN KILT

Tracey wanted me to make a wrap skirt, but I resisted because I kept imagining it opening and exposing our thighs at awkward moments. So we decided to compromise by working a skirt in the round but adding a flirty vertical panel to the front. The panel at the hem is knitted as one long piece, with short rows to give it some flare. We both love linen. It drapes so beautifully and is heaven to knit. Ⓜ

TRACEY SAYS: *I'm very proud of my contributions to this design. I made sure that the ribbed top section ended mid-buttock to distract and minimize.*

SIZES
One size

FINISHED MEASUREMENTS
32 ³/₄" (83.2 cm) waist (before adding elastic); 40" (101.6 cm) hips; 27" (68.6 cm) long

YARN
Euroflax Linen (100% linen; 270 yards (247 meters) / 100 grams): 4 skeins #89 quarry stone

NEEDLES
One pair straight needles size US 5 (3.75 mm)

One 36" (91 cm) circular (circ) needle size US 5 (3.75 mm)

One 29" (74 cm) circular needle size US 4 (3.5 mm)

Change needle size if necessary to obtain correct gauge.

NOTIONS
Crochet hook size F/5 (3.75 mm)

Contrasting sewing thread; 1 yard 1" elastic

GAUGE
21 sts and 26 rows = 4" (10 cm) in Stockinette stitch (St st) using larger needles

NOTES
Bottom Ruffle is worked sideways and is shaped using short rows.

When stitching turned hems on the WS, be careful to catch the part of the st that is closest to the WS surface. This will make the hemline less visible on the RS.

For an explanation of ribbing in different multiples of knit and purl stitches, see page 165.

BOTTOM RUFFLE

Using larger needles, cast on 36 sts.

Establish Pattern:

Rows 1 and 3 (RS): Knit.

Rows 2 and 4: Purl.

Row 5: K27, turn.

Rows 6 and 8: Purl.

Row 7: K25, turn.

Rows 9-12: Work in St st, beginning with a knit row.

Rows 13-16: Work in Reverse St st, beginning with a purl row.

Row 17: P27, turn.

Rows 18 and 20: Knit.

Row 19: P25, turn.

Rows 21-24: Work in Reverse St st, beginning with a purl row.

Repeat Rows 1-24 18 times.

Bind off all sts knitwise. Sew cast-on edge to bound-off edge.

SKIRT

Using larger circ needle, beginning at Bottom Ruffle seam, pick up and knit 210 sts along shorter edge of Bottom Ruffle. *NOTE: You will pick up 11 stitches for each 24-row repeat of the Bottom Ruffle, and 1 extra st halfway along the Ruffle.* Join for working in the rnd, being careful not to twist sts; place marker (pm) for beginning of rnd. Begin St st.

Work even until piece measures 12" from pick-up row (approximately 18" from beginning).

Shape Skirt:

Decrease Rnd: K4, ssk, k1, k2tog, *k9, ssk, k1, k2tog; repeat from * to last 5 sts, k5—180 sts remain.

Change to smaller circ needle and 1x1 Rib. Work even for 5".

Shape Waistband: Purl 1 rnd. Knit 10 rnds. Purl 1 rnd (fold line). Knit 10 rnds. Bind off all sts.

VERTICAL RUFFLE

Using contrasting thread, baste a vertical line up Skirt from beginning of Bottom Ruffle seam to beginning of ribbing. Using crochet hook, work single crochet along this line.

RS facing, using larger needles, pick up and knit 84 stitches evenly along chain.

(WS) Begin 6x6 Rib, as follows: *K6, p6; repeat from * across. Work even for 7 rows.

Increase Row 1 (RS): *K3, m1, k3, p6; repeat from * to end—91 sts.

Increase Row 2 (WS): *K3, m1, k3, p7; repeat from * to end—98 sts.

Work even in 7x7 Rib as established for 6 rows.

Increase Row 3 (RS): *K4, m1, k3, p7; repeat from * to end—105 sts.

Increase Row 4 (WS): *K4, m1, k3, p8; repeat from * to end—112 sts.

Work even in 8x8 Rib as established for 6 rows.

Bind off all sts in pattern.

Sew edge of Vertical Panel along base of Waistband.

Measure your waist. Cut length of elastic 1" shorter than waist measurement and sew ends together. Fold Waistband over elastic to WS and and sew in place, being careful not to let sts show on WS.

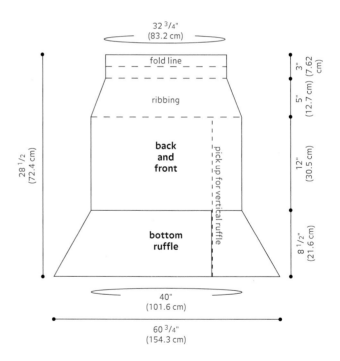

MURIWAI BATH MAT

Muriwai is a wild and windy beach on the west coast of New Zealand. I once visited a house there that had a bathroom with a view of the ocean, and I fancied lying in the bath, looking out the window. This is the kind of mat I'd like to step onto after just such a long soak. The Muriwai is knitted with a double strand of a ropelike cotton yarn. First you work a rectangle, then you pick up stitches around the edges, then you knit around and around, increasing at the corners. When the mat is the size you like, you finish with a picot bind off. **M**

FINISHED MEASUREMENTS
28" (71.1 cm) x 36" (91.4 cm)

YARN
Rowan Cotton Rope (55% cotton / 45% acrylic: 63 yards (58 meters) / 50 grams): 16 balls #067 white

NEEDLES
One 24" (60 cm) circular (circ) needle size US 10 1/2 (6.5 mm)

One 32" (80 cm) circular needle size US 10 1/2 (6.5 mm)

One 40" (100 cm) circular needle size US 10 1/2 (6.5 mm)

Change needle size if necessary to obtain correct gauge.

NOTIONS
Stitch markers

GAUGE
12 sts and 16 rows = 4" (10 cm) in Stockinette st (St st) using 2 strands of yarn held together

NOTES
If you want to make a smaller Bath Mat, follow the instructions as written but end increases when Mat is desired dimension and st count is a multiple of 5. Complete Picot Edge as written.

Using 24" long circ needle and 2 strands of yarn held together, cast on 20 sts.

Work even in St st for 50 rows, beginning with a purl row. Bind off all sts.

RS facing, using 24" long circ needle and 2 strands of yarn held together, and beginning in corner, pick up and knit 124 sts as follows: 40 sts across long side, place marker (pm), 1 st at corner, pm, 20 sts across short side, pm, 1 st at corner, pm, 40 sts across long side, pm, 1 st at corner, pm, 20 sts across short side, pm, 1 st at corner. Join for working in the rnd, pm for beginning of rnd.

Establish Pattern:

Rnd 1: Purl.

Rnd 2: *M1, knit to marker, m1, slip marker (sm), k1, sm; repeat from * to end—132 sts.

Repeat Rnds 1 and 2 until there are 340 sts, ending with Rnd 1.

Work Picot Edging:

*Using Knitted Cast-On (see page 164), cast on 1 st. Bind off 6 sts. Transfer st from right-hand needle back to left-hand needle. Repeat from * to last corner st, cast on 1 st, bind off remaining 2 sts. Weave in ends.

TAHITI-STYLE PHOTO FRAMES

The vibrant flowers of South Pacific islands inspired me to design these Stockinette-stitch photo frames with mitered corners and optional bougainvillea-inspired knitted flower or shell-button embellishments. They're designed to fit a Plexiglas box frame. The rustic Habu silk reminds me of coconut fiber or tree bark, and gives the frame the look of weathered wood. The flowers are made of bamboo yarn in the colors of the tropics. Make one to show off a favorite holiday snapshot. Ⓜ
TRACEY ADDS: *I want to knit a tartan frame to show off a snap of my husband teeing off at St Andrews in Scotland. A painstaking gift from a veteran golf widow.*

SIZES
Small (Large)

FINISHED MEASUREMENTS
To fit a 5 x 7 x 1½ (8 x 10 x 1½)" (12.7 x 17.8 x 3.8 (20.3 x 25.4 x 3.8) cm) plastic box frame

YARN
Habu Textiles Tsumugi Silk Combination A-111 (100% silk; 156 yards (141 meters) / 56 grams): 1 ball for each size frame

Shown in the following colors:
#HA1 green or #2 gray (A) for Small; #8 brick for Large (A)

Small amounts of fingering weight yarn for flowers (B) (optional)

Flowers shown in Alchemy Bamboo (100% bamboo; 138 yards (126.2 meters) / 50 grams) in the following colors: #068W mist, #066E willow, #80A evening pink, #39A fuchsia, #38R Clio's fancy, #45S koi pond

NEEDLES
Small Frame: One 16" (40 cm) circular (circ) needle size US 5 (3.75 mm)

Large Frame: One 29" (74 cm) circular needle size US 5 (3.75 mm)

One pair straight needles size US 2 (3 mm) for flowers (optional)

Change needle size if necessary to obtain correct gauge.

NOTIONS
Stitch markers; plastic box frame 5 x 7 x 1½ (8 x 10 x 1½)"; various mother of pearl or shell buttons, up to 1" (optional)

GAUGE
20 sts = 4" (10 cm) in Stockinette st (St st) using larger needle

FRAME

Using larger needles and A, cast on 88 (128) sts. Join for working in the rnd, being careful not to twist sts; place marker (pm) for beginning of rnd.

Rnd 1: K8 (12), pm, k28 (40), pm, k16 (24), pm, k28 (40), pm, k8 (12).

Rnd 2: *K2, yo, k2tog; repeat from * to end of rnd.

Rnd 3: *Knit to marker, kfb, sm, kfb; repeat from * 3 times, knit to end—96 (136) sts.

Rnd 4: Knit.

Rnds 5-10: Repeat Rnds 3 and 4—120 (160) sts after Rnd 9.

Rnds 11-17: Knit.

Rnd 18: *Knit to 2 sts before marker, ssk, sm, k2tog; repeat from * 3 times, knit to end—112 (152) sts remain.

Rnd 19: Knit.

Rnds 20-27: Repeat Rnds 18 and 19—80 (120) sts remain after Rnd 26.

Size Large Only:

Rnds 28-29: Repeat Rnds 18 and 19—112 sts remain after Rnd 28.

Both Sizes: Bind off all sts purlwise.

FLOWERS (optional)
Make several in colors as desired.

Using smaller needles and B, cast on 3 sts.

Row 1 (RS): Kfb, knit to end—4 sts.

Row 2: K2, purl to end.

Rows 3-4: Repeat Rows 1 and 2—5 sts after Row 3.

Row 5: Repeat Row 1—6 sts.

Row 6: K2, purl to end.

Row 7: Bind off 4 sts, kfb—3 sts remain.

Repeat Rows 2-7 three times. Repeat Rows 2-6 once. Bind off all stitches.

Break yarn, leaving a 12" tail. Thread tail through edges of Garter st ridges along straight side of Flower. Pull tight, arrange in a circle, and fasten off.

FINISHING
Sew buttons or Flowers to Frame (see photos).

Using A, make a Twisted Cord 30 (40)" long (see page 165). Starting at mid-point of top edge of Frame, thread Cord through eyelets, slip Frame over plastic frame, pull Cord to tighten, tie bow to secure. Securing with a bow rather than a knot will allow you to easily change frame contents.

Keep leftover yarns for scarves or embellishments.

Knitty Dreads

In the 1980s, I wore green and orange nylon-fiber dreadlocks in my hair. A fellow called Simon at a cool London hair salon called Antenna attached them to my head. Boy George and Adam Ant went there, too.

I loved my dreadlocks. They shocked people. I would turn up at my husband's golf tournaments wearing a Sex Pistols T-shirt and would shake my head menacingly at the other wives, who held their blond bobs back with velvet headbands. I could tie them up, wear them loose, change the colors, spike them—they were great fun—but eventually I tired of them, as they did have a tendency to fall out at inappropriate moments, or get caught in friends' earrings as we air-kissed.

Recently, I bumped into a musician friend I had not seen in ages, and he had a full head of natural dreadlocks. He'd spent several years achieving this splendid look. "You should do it, Tracey," he said, "You're getting a little staid-looking." That shook me as I have never been one to conform, but I like my long, shiny hair with its traces of gray, and it feels good to be able to run a comb through my tresses.

I wanted some versatility but without the sacrifice. So I went to my knitting basket and found some lovely brown Koigu yarn and multicolored ribbon. I knitted lots of thin strips with the brown yarn and braided them three at a time. Next I stitched the strips together at one end and wrapped them with the ribbon. Finally, I put the strips through a hair elastic, tied my hair in a topknot, and let the strips cascade around my face. Instead of taking years of twisting and matting my own hair, the whole knitted look had only taken a couple of hours.

Here I am looking like George Clinton of Funkadelic, as sponsored by Koigu. ⓣ

SOUTH SEAS TABLE RUNNER

What table doesn't need a pretty runner? This one is worked in sportweight linen in an openwork stitch that resembles cane work. The shell buttons at the corners give it a hint of the sea. **M**
TRACEY ADDS: You could make this in a larger size and hang it in a doorway for dramatic entrances and exits.

FINISHED MEASUREMENTS
13" (33 cm) wide x 30" (76.2 cm) long

YARN
Euroflax Originals (100% linen; 270 yards (247 meters) / 100 grams): 1 hank #18.47 terra cotta

NEEDLES
One pair straight needles size US 4 (3.5 mm)

Change needle size if necessary to obtain correct gauge.

NOTIONS
18 9/16" flat shell beads

GAUGE
16 sts and 23 rows = 4" (10 cm) in Stockinette st (St st)

NOTES
You can make a longer runner by using an extra hank of yarn and continuing the repeat until you reach the desired length.

To achieve a neat finish with Garter st, after knitting the first st of the row, put your needle into the second st and give the yarn a tug to pull it tight before completing the second st.

TABLE RUNNER
Cast on 52 sts; knit 4 rows.

Establish Pattern:

Row 1 (RS) : K2, *k2, [yo] twice, k2; repeat from * to last 2 sts, k2—76 sts.

Row 2: K2, *p2tog, p1 (yo from previous row), k1 (yo from previous row), p2tog; repeat from * to last 2 sts, k2—52 sts remain.

Row 3: K2, yo, *k4, [yo] twice; repeat from * to last 6 sts, k4, yo, k2—76 sts.

Row 4: K2, p1, *[p2tog] twice, p1 (yo from previous row), k1 (yo from previous row); repeat from * to last 7 sts, [p2tog] twice, p1, k2—52 sts remain.

Repeat Rows 1-4 forty times, then repeat Rows 1 and 2 once.

Knit 4 rows.

Bind off all sts. Weave in ends.

Lightly block using a damp cloth.

Split a length of yarn and use a single strand to sew beads in clusters of 3 at corners and in the center of both ends.

knit2together
43

SAUCY APRON

I love aprons, vintage and new, and some are too pretty to hide in the kitchen. My mother once mistakenly wore one to town for an outing with a group of toddlers. She must have been too busy to notice, until she looked down at her lap on the bus ride home. I always wear an apron when I'm cooking and, recently, I've seen them worn over jeans, like a half-skirt. Why not? My mother did! **M** TRACEY POINTS OUT: *Purely a fashion item. Wouldn't want to splash this adorable little number with hot fat or beet juice.*

FINISHED MEASUREMENTS
35" (88.9 cm) wide x 19" (48.3 cm) long

YARN
GGH Soft Kid (70% super kid mohair / 25% nylon / 5% wool; 151 yards (138 meters) / 25 grams): 3 balls #13 violet (A), 2 balls #74 peach (B), 1 ball #76 green (C)

NEEDLES
One 24" (60 cm) circular (circ) needle size US 5 (3.75 mm)

Change needle size if necessary to obtain correct gauge.

NOTIONS
Crochet hook size F/5 (3.75 mm) (optional)

Stitch markers; 2 pieces of cardboard, each 1 1/2" square for Pompoms

GAUGE
26 sts and 32 rows = 4" (10 cm) in 11x6 Rib, slightly stretched

NOTES
For an explanation of ribbing in different multiples of knit and purl stitches, see page 165.

APRON

Using B, cast on 227 sts; begin 11x6 Rib, as follows: P6, *k11, p6; repeat from * across. Next row (WS): Knit the knit sts and purl the purl sts as they face you. Work even until piece measures 4" from beginning, ending with a WS row.

Shape Apron: Change to A.

Decrease Row 1 (RS): *P6, skp, k7, k2tog; repeat from * to last 6 sts, p6—201 sts remain.

Decrease Row 2: *K2, k2tog, k2, p9; repeat from * to last 6 sts, k2, k2tog, k2—187 sts remain.

Next Row (RS): *P5, k9; repeat from * to last 5 sts, p5.

Work even in 5x9 Rib as established until piece measures 9 1/4" from the beginning, ending with a WS row.

Decrease Row 3 (RS): *P5, skp, k5, k2tog; repeat from * to last 5 sts, p5—161 sts remain.

Decrease Row 4: *K2, k2tog, k1, p7; repeat from * to last 5 sts, k2, k2tog, k1—147 sts remain.

Next Row (RS): *P4, k7; repeat from * to last 4 sts, p4.

Work even in 4x7 Rib as established until piece measures 19" from the beginning, ending with a WS row.

Bind off all sts in pattern.

WAISTBAND

Using B, cast on 15 sts; begin 1x1 Rib, as follows: K1, *p1, k1; repeat from * across. Next row (WS): Knit the knit sts and purl the purl sts as they face you. Work even until piece measures 54" from the beginning.

Bind off all sts in pattern. Fold Waistband in half lengthwise. Place one marker 6" to either side of fold for finishing.

POCKET

Using B, cast on 40 sts; begin 7x4 Rib, as follows: K7, *p4, k7; repeat from * across. Next row (WS): Knit the knit sts and purl the purl sts as they face you. Work even until piece measures 2" from the beginning, ending with a WS row.

Decrease Row (RS): *Ssk, k3, k2tog, p4; repeat to last 7 sts, ssk, k3, k2tog—32 sts remain.

Next Row (WS): *P5, k4; repeat from * to last 5 sts, p5.

Work even in 5x4 Rib as established until piece measures 3 1/2" from the beginning, ending with a WS row.

Next Row (RS): Change to A. Knit 1 row.

(WS): Change to 5x4 Rib. Work even until piece measures 5" from the beginning, ending with a WS row. Pm each side for cuff.

(RS): Work even until piece measures 6 1/2" from beginning.

Bind off all sts in pattern.

FINISHING

Side Ruffle: RS facing, using C, pick up and knit 98 sts along side edge of Apron.

Row 1 (WS): *K3, p2; repeat from * to last 3 sts, k3.

Row 2: *P3, k1, m1, k1; repeat from * to last 3 sts, p3—117 sts.

Row 3: *K3, p3; repeat from * to last 3 sts, k3.

Row 4: *P3, k1, m1, k1, m1, k1; repeat from * to last 3 sts, p3—155 sts.

Row 5: *K3, p5; repeat from * to last 3 sts, k3.

Row 6: *P3, k1, m1, k3, m1, k1; repeat from * to last 3 sts, p3—193 sts.

Row 7: *K3, p7; repeat from * to last 3 sts, k3.

Row 8: *P3, k7; repeat from * to last 3 sts, p3.

Row 9: *K3, p7; repeat from * to last 3 sts, k3.

Bind off all sts in pattern.

Repeat for other side of Apron.

Sew Waistband to Apron, easing top of Apron between markers on Waistband. Fold cuff of Pocket to RS at markers and pin to Pocket. Sew Pocket to Apron 2 1/2" below Waistband and 3" from outer edge of Ruffle on right side of Apron, stitching edges of cuff to Apron.

Pompoms: Make one 1 1/2" Pompom (see page 164) in each color. Make one 1" crochet chain (see page 164) in each color, leaving 6" tail at beginning and end of chain. Attach chain to Pompom; attach opposite end of chain to bottom edge of contrasting Pocket trim.

Sew a long tail of yarn into the side seam of a sweater and you'll always have mending material.

I've Never Played Betty Crocker

No, I am not that kind of mother, and my children are very aware of this. I cannot cook, apart from boiling pasta. What's the point? Until the age of twelve most kids refuse to eat anything but yellow food anyway. When my children were younger I was useless at helping with school art projects. We were the family who made the pathetic last-minute dioramas that were laughed at on Monday mornings, the ones with Pilgrim Fathers with plasticine sausage arms that fell off as soon as the school bus hit the first bump. I never set up a cupboard full of glue sticks, poster board, crepe paper, and glitter. My daughter, Mabel, remembers going to a friend's house in the fourth grade and being amazed to see that her friend's mother kept cereal in Tupperware containers and Popsicle sticks in a designated "Crafts Drawer."

"Why can't you carve pumpkins and dip Easter eggs?" Mabel asked. "Why do you wear wigs, rubber chins, and chest hair?" Playing dress up—now that was the one area where other mothers couldn't even begin to compete with me. And nobody improvised Barbie scenarios like me. I could twitter on for hours about getting my new dune buggy, and how Ken was embarrassing me by wearing flared Lurex pants. I was able to give Malibu Barbie a totally different persona to that of Ballerina Barbie—no mean feat.

Then, suddenly, when Mabel started college and Johnny hit junior high I surprised everyone by picking up knitting needles and producing book bags, mittens, and socks. The kids were wary at first, and there was one ugly moment when I was accused of paying a professional costume designer to produce these items! But after a live demonstration of knit and purl stitches with a skein of cashmere and some bamboo needles, they believed me and soon started requesting sweaters and enjoying saying things like, "Oh, my Mum made this. She does things like this all the time." I did have to warn them that knitting was probably the most "mumsy" thing I was ever going to do, that gingerbread houses, Jell-O molds, and Popsicle sticks wouldn't necessarily follow, and they seemed content with that. But recently I found myself experimenting with an apple pie recipe, my first since home-economics class in 1972. I don't know what's come over me (perimenopause, I suspect) but if this continues, I don't think I can rule out creating my very own Crafts Drawer for the grandchildren. ⓣ

HOUSE SLIPPERS

These felted slippers are a snip (easy and fast) to make and even more fun to embellish with embroidery, beads, buttons, or whatever other adornments you can dream up. The felted adornments shown here are made by felting a Stockinette-stitch swatch, then cutting out shapes, such as bows or flowers. A line of these at the front door should encourage family and friends to remove their shoes, make themselves at home, and stick around for a while. **Ⓜ** TRACEY SAYS: *Anything to stop my son from walking through the house in mud-caked soccer boots.*

SIZES
To fit women's <men's> shoe size 5–7 (7–9, 9–11) <3¹/₂–5¹/₂ (5¹/₂–7¹/₂, 7¹/₂–9¹/₂)>
Shown in all sizes

FINISHED MEASUREMENTS
Sole before felting: 5 (5, 5¹/₂)" wide x 11 (11¹/₂, 11¹/₂)" long; after felting 3¹/₂ (3¹/₂, 4)" wide x 9 (9¹/₂, 10)" long

YARN
Yarn 1: Manos del Uruguay Wool (100% wool; 138 yards (126.2 meters) / 100 grams): 2 hanks of A, 1 hank of B
Yarn 2: Rio de La Plata Wool (100% wool; 140 yards (128 meters) / 100 grams): 2 hanks of A, 1 hank of B; mix and match as desired or use colors shown
Yarn colors and slipper sizes:
See page 50

NEEDLES
One pair straight needles size US 13 (9 mm)
One 24" (60 cm) circular (circ) needle size US 11 (8 mm)
Change needle size if necessary to obtain correct gauge.

NOTIONS
2 removable markers in different colors; stitch marker; contrasting scrap yarn; embroidery thread and buttons (optional); ¹/₃ yard velvet ribbon (optional)

GAUGE
8 ³/₄ sts and 17 rows = 4" (10 cm) in Garter st using larger needles and 3 strands of yarn held together

NOTE
The Slipper is worked using 3 strands of yarn held together (see Technique on page 50)

SLIPPER (make 2)
SOLE
Using larger needles and 3 strands of A held together, cast on 5 (5, 6) sts; begin Garter st, increase 1 st each side on the second and fourth rows—9 (9, 10) sts. Work even for 22 (24, 24) rows.

(RS) Increase 1 st each side—11 (11, 12) sts. Place a removable marker in base of first and last sts to mark top side (inside) of Slipper. Work even for 15 rows.

Shape Toe: (RS) Decrease 1 st each side every other row 3 times as follows: Skp, work to last 2 sts, k2tog—5 (5, 6) sts remain. Bind off all sts knitwise.

LIP
With top side of Sole (marker side) facing, using circ needle and 3 strands of A held together, beginning 1 (1, 2) Garter st ridges to left of second marker, pick up and knit 29 (31, 30) sts around heel to 1 (1, 2) Garter st ridges before first marker, pick up and knit 1 (1, 2) sts to first marker, 27 (27, 28) sts around toe to second marker, then 1 (1, 2) sts to beginning of rnd—58 (60, 62) sts. Join for working in the rnd; place marker for beginning of rnd. Purl 1 rnd.

Shape Heel: Continuing in Garter st, bind off 29 (31, 30) sts knitwise, work to end—29 (29, 32) sts remain.

Next Row: Skp, work to last 2 sts, k2tog—27 (27, 30) sts remain.

Slipper Upper: Transfer next 11 (11, 12) sts to right-hand end of circ needle, transfer next 5 (5, 6) sts at toe to larger straight needle (with tip of needle pointing to the left); leave remaining 11 (11, 12) sts on left-hand end of circ needle. Break yarn.

MAKING A TRIPLE BALL

Note: A swift, ball winder and kitchen scale are particularly useful for this.

To wind yarn from two hanks into a triple ball, first wind two hanks of A into 2 separate center-pull balls. To make a triple ball, take the outside and inside ends of one ball, and the outside end from the second ball, and wind the 3 strands together into one large ball, cutting the yarn from the second ball when the triple ball is complete.

To wind yarn from a single hank into a triple ball, first weigh the hank; divide the weight by one third, then wind one third of the hank into a ball, stopping to weigh the ball as you go. Break the yarn. Wind the remaining yarn into a single center-pull ball. Take the smaller ball and the 2 ends from the center-pull ball, and wind together into a triple ball as above.

SLIPPER COLORS & SIZES

YARN 1:
MANOS DEL URUGUAY WOOL

Slipper 1: Size Large, using #59 kohl (A) and #48 cherry (B), with lattice embroidery and buttons.

Slipper 2: Size Medium, using #70 spring (A) and #4 turquoise (B), with zigzag embroidery.

Slipper 4: Size Small, using #17 cheek (A) and #O rose (B), with flower and button.

YARN 2:
RÍO DE LA PLATA WOOL

Slipper 3: Size Medium, using #A46 crabapple (A) and #A10 fuchsia (B), with bow.

Slipper 5: Size Small, using #A36 coral (A) and #A15 pale blue pastel (B), with ribbon and button.

Slipper 6: Size Small, using #A40 ethereal blue (A) and #A7 red orange (B), with flower.

Slipper 7 (shown on page 37): Size Medium, using #A46 crabapple and Manos del Uruguay #47 fuschia, with flower.

NOTE: RS will be outside of Slipper upper.

Establish Toe: Row 1 (RS): Change to Stockinette stitch and 3 strands of B held together; k5 (5, 6) sts from straight needle, k1 from circ needle, turn—6 (6, 7) sts on straight needle.

Row 2: P6 (6, 7), p1 from circ needle, turn—7 (7, 8) sts; 10 (10, 11) sts remain each side on circ needle.

Work even as established for 4 rows, working 1 st from circ needle at end of each row—11 (11, 12) sts on straight needle; 8 (8, 9) sts remain each side on circ needle.

Shape Instep:

Row 1: (RS) Knit to last st on needle, k2tog [last st with 1 st from circ needle], turn.

Row 2: Purl to last st on needle, p2tog [last st with 1 st from circ needle], turn—7 (7, 8) sts remain each side on circ needle.

Repeat Rows 1 and 2 5 (5, 6) times, then repeat Row 1 three times; 1 st remains on right end of circ needle.

(WS) Bind off 9 (9, 10) sts knitwise, p2tog [last st with 1 st from circ needle], bind off 1 st. Fasten off. Remove markers. Weave end into Lip.

FLOWER/BOW SQUARES (make 2)

Using larger needles and single strand of A, cast on 20 sts; begin St st. Work even until piece is as long as it is wide. Bind off all sts.

FINISHING
FELTING

Wash Slippers and Squares in hot water and detergent in a washing machine, with a towel for friction. Stretch Slippers as necessary to fit foot; stuff toes with paper towels until they are dry.

Using leftover yarn, embellish slippers as in photos.

Flowers: (optional) Cut 2 circles 1 3/4" in diameter from edge of one felted square, leaving room to cut Bows (see below). Cut 2 circles 1 1/4" in diameter from edge of second felted square.

Steam press these 4 circles flat. Place smaller circle on top of larger circle, then sew to Slippers. Embroider edges of circles or attach button (optional).

Bows: (optional) Cut 2 bow shapes 2 1/2" x 1" from remainder of felted squares. Wind contrasting yarn several times around center; sew in place on Slipper.

Embroidery: (optional) Mark out lattice or zigzag pattern with pins and embroider with a running stitch.

Every Man Needs a Quiver

One of my early efforts was a felted spectacle case for my husband. In my rush to complete it for Christmas, I did not check the gauge and the size of the needles (a classic beginner's mistake) and the piece came out far too big. Even after I had washed it in very hot water several times, it still had not shrunk sufficiently. I gave it to him anyway and said that it was an arrow case, something every manly man should own. Now I have to knit him a target. **T**

SEA ANEMONE MESSENGER BAG

I love to carry a messenger bag because I can sling it across my body and not worry about the strap falling off my shoulder. This one is knitted in one piece from the base up; bright tentacles are knitted onto the flap; then the whole thing is felted. **M**

FINISHED MEASUREMENTS
Bag: Approximately 30" (76.2 cm) circumference x 12" (30.5 cm) high after felting

Strap: Approximately 36" (91.4 cm) long after felting

YARN
Cascade 220 (100% wool; 220 yards (201 meters) / 100 grams): 3 hanks each #9323 dark spruce heather (A) and #8229 country green (B), 1 hank #9444 tangerine heather (C)

NEEDLES
One 24" (60 cm) circular (circ) needle size US 13 (9 mm)

One pair double-pointed needles (dpn) size US 8 (5 mm)

Change needle size if necessary to obtain correct gauge.

NOTIONS
Stitch markers, including 1 in contrasting color; stitch holders

GAUGE
9 sts and 13 rows = 4" (10 cm) on largest needles, using 2 strands of yarn held together.

NOTES
The Bag is worked using 2 strands of yarn held together. The Embellishments are worked using a single strand of yarn.

BASE

Using larger needle and 2 strands of A held together, cast on 18 sts; begin Garter st. Work 1 row.

Shape Base: Kfb, knit to last st, kfb—20 sts. Work even until piece measures 11" from the beginning.

Next Row: Ssk, work to last 2 sts, k2tog—18 sts remain.

Knit 1 row.

Bind off all sts.

BAG

Using larger needle and 2 strands of A held together, pick up and knit 112 sts, as follows: 20 sts along first short side of Base, place marker (pm), 1 st in corner, pm, 34 sts along long side, pm, 1 st in corner, pm, 20 sts along second short side, pm, 1 st in corner, pm, 34 sts along remaining side, pm, 1 st in corner. Join for working in the rnd; pm (contrasting color) for beginning of rnd.

Rnd 1: Knit.

Rnd 2: Knit, slipping all corner sts purlwise wyib.

Repeat Rnds 1 and 2 until piece measures 8" from pick-up rnd.

NOTE: When working decrease rnds, continue to knit or slip corner sts as established, depending on the row you are working on.

Shape Bag: Decrease Rnd 1: Slip marker (sm), *ssk, k16, k2tog, sm, work corner st, sm, k34, sm, work corner st, sm; repeat from * around—108 sts remain.

Work even until piece measures 15 1/4" from pick-up rnd.

Decrease Rnd 2: Change to B; sm, *ssk, k14, k2tog, sm, work corner st, sm, k34, sm, work corner st, sm; repeat from * around—104 sts remain.

I Did It My Way . . . At First

One day at Wildfiber I was drawn to a gorgeous little handbag Mel had made out of a tweedy silk yarn from Habu Textiles. It was about six inches wide and deep, was laced together on four sides with a contrasting yarn, and was held with lovely wooden handles. I immediately got that "Oooh, I want to knit that!" feeling—accompanied by moist palms, dry mouth, and a tingling in the abdomen. Sounds similar to something else, doesn't it?

I had to make this bag! But I am not one for dainty little purses that accommodate two aspirins and a junior Tampax. I like roomy totes that can hold scripts, tap shoes, a small spaniel even. So I cleared the shelf of the remaining skeins, paid quickly, and rushed home with my new love. I was sure my larger version of Mel's design was going to be fabulous. I quickly cast on three times as many stitches as Mel had, and began imagining myself embarking on weekends in the country with my sturdy traveling companion.

The yarn was grainy and tough, and after a few rows my fingers tingled and glowed, but I was enjoying the challenge. I knitted long past midnight. "Turn out the light," my husband grumbled around one in the morning—but I was possessed. At about two I had completed two slanted eighteen-inch sides with carefully placed holes for lacing together later. I decided to take a rest. I awoke early the next morning with blisters on my index fingers but I was unfazed. I wrapped them in Band-Aids and picked up my needles. "Project fever" possessed me. I wasn't eating or answering the phone, and when I did get up, I was wandering around the house in my pajamas, trailing yarn.

By late afternoon the base and four sides lay in front of me, and it was time to stitch them up. I grasped a yarn needle and started to lace through the holes. But something was amiss. Instead of standing to attention to receive books and dogs, my bag sagged alarmingly in the middle. I poked and prodded and even shouted at it, but to no avail.

How stupid I'd been! There was a reason Mel had kept her bag small. The stiffness of the silk could only hold up at those proportions. It was like a physics calculation I had gotten horribly wrong. My new love had turned into a monster I wanted to stuff behind the hot water tank and forget about. But Mel knew I was making it and would surely ask me how it was coming along. Perhaps I could say it had been stolen or washed away in a freak wave when I was knitting at the beach.

There was nothing for me to do but get dressed and drive to Wildfiber to request an emergency consultation. Luckily, there was no one else in the shop as Mel held up my bag like a floppy fish. "I've got an idea," she said, and started to rummage through the oddments box she keeps on the counter. "We can pinch in the four corners and thread ribbon through. This will square it off and add stiffness." She produced some contrasting ribbon and, before I knew it, the floppy fish was standing to attention. The ribbon had not only improved the bag but had made it into a unique design that looked fantastic. Tears of relief welled in my eyes. The salvaging operation had been a success, and I owed it to Mel.

I immediately filled my new bag with some gorgeous balls of yarn. Forget the scripts and the spaniel. I didn't want to put undue strain on my near disaster. I have used it as my knitting bag ever since. **ⓣ**

Work even until piece measures 19 ½" from pick-up rnd.

Next Rnd: Sm, k16, sm, k1, sm, p34, knit to end, slipping all markers.

Next Rnd: Knit.

Next Rnd: Sm, k16, sm, k1, sm, p34 , knit to end, slipping all markers.

Next Rnd: K17, bind off 34 sts for Bag opening, knit to end, removing all markers—70 sts remain.

STRAP

Next Row (RS): K17, place remaining 53 sts on holder for Flap and second Strap.

(WS) Working back and forth on needle, bind off 1 st purlwise, purl to end—16 sts remain.

(RS) Continuing in St st, work even until Strap measures 25" from the beginning, ending with a RS row. Place sts on holder.

RS facing, rejoin yarn to 17 sts at opposite end of Bag opening (this will include one corner slip st next to bound-off edge);

leave remaining 36 sts on holder for Flap. Bind off 1 st, k15—16 sts remain.

Complete as for first Strap, ending with a WS row. Graft Strap sts together using Kitchener st (see page 164).

FLAP

RS facing, rejoin yarn to remaining sts on holder.

Beginning with a knit row, work even in St st for 4 rows, binding off 1 st at beginning of first 2 rows—34 sts remain.

Establish Eyelet Pattern:

Row 1 (RS): K2, *yo, k2tog, k2; repeat from * to end.

Rows 2-6: Work in St st, beginning with a purl row.

Row 7: K4, *yo, k2tog, k2; repeat from * to last 2 sts, k2.

Rows 8-12: Repeat Rows 2-6.

Repeat Rows 1-12 four times. Repeat Rows 1-6 once.

Bind off all sts.

FINISHING

Flap Edging: RS facing, using larger needle and 2 strands of yarn held together, beginning at top of Flap, pick up and knit 38 sts along first side, 1 st in corner, 32 sts along bottom edge, 1 st in corner, and 38 sts along second side—110 sts.

Bind off all sts knitwise.

Weave in ends.

Embellishments: Using dpn and single strand of C, cast on 3 sts; work I-cord (see page 164) 3" long. Work 75 Embellishments (one for each eyelet on the Flap). Sew Embellishments into eyelets, securing so that end of I-cord is flush with Flap. Weave in ends.

FELTING

Wash Bag in very hot water and detergent in a washing machine, together with a dry towel for friction. Wash a second time if Bag has not felted adequately after first washing. Stuff Bag with paper towels until dry.

LUXE NECK WARMER

I knitted one of these cashmere neck pieces one evening at home, wore it to work the next day, and then it quickly became one of the most popular projects at Wildfiber. Knitted in the classic feather-and-fan stitch on size 10 needles, it serves the same purpose as a scarf but is much quicker to make and easier to wear. Ⓜ TRACEY SAYS: *Pull it up over your nose when skiing, or traveling incognito.*

FINISHED MEASUREMENTS
19¹/₂" (49.5 cm) circumference x 9" (22.9 cm) long

YARN
Classic Elite Yarns Sinful (100% cashmere; 65 yards (59 meters) / 50 grams): 2 hanks #20093 natural or #92606 aqua

NEEDLES
One 16" (40 cm) circular needle size US 10 (6 mm)

Change needle size if necessary to obtain correct gauge.

NOTIONS
Stitch marker

GAUGE
14³/₄ sts and 22³/₄ rows = 4" (10 cm) in Feather-and-Fan Stitch

NECK WARMER

Using Cable Cast-On method (see page 164), cast on 72 sts. Join for working in the rnd, being careful not to twist sts, place marker (pm) for beginning of rnd. Begin Feather-and-Fan Stitch.

Work even until nearly all yarn is used, or piece measures 9" from the beginning, ending with Rnd 4, leaving enough yarn to bind off. Bind off all sts.

STITCH PATTERN

FEATHER-AND-FAN STITCH

(multiple of 12 sts; 4-row repeat)

Rnd 1: Knit.

Rnd 2: [K2tog] twice, *[yo, k1] 4 times, [k2tog] 4 times; repeat from * to last 8 sts, [yo, k1] 4 times, [k2tog] twice.

Rnd 3: Purl.

Rnd 4: Knit.

Repeat Rnds 1-4 for Feather-and-Fan Stitch.

Place a number of knots in the tail of a swatch as a reminder of what size needle you used.

GYM SLIP DRESS

At my high school in New Zealand, all the girls were required to wear a uniform called a gym slip (a tunic worn at the knee and not an inch shorter). The purpose of the gym slip was to make everyone look the same, but we always found ways to spice it up with saucy items like hot pink witches britches (knickers that reached almost to the knee; see page 62) edged with black lace. This is my fantasy gym slip, so much more stylish than the original. Knitted in the round from the bottom up, it begins with a panel of ruching at the hem, followed by Stockinette stitch, then a lace panel at the waist, and 5-by-1 ribbing at the bodice. If desired, instead of working the lace, you can knit the waist in Stockinette stitch. **M**

SIZES
Small (Medium, Large)
Shown in size Small

FINISHED MEASUREMENTS
32 (34, 37 1/2)" (81.3 (86.4, 95.3) cm)

YARN
Jaegar Extra Fine Merino (100% extra fine merino; 136 yards (124 meters) / 50 grams): 12 (14,16) balls #978 coal dust (MC); 2 (3, 3) balls #951 jet (A)

NEEDLES
One 36" (91 cm) circular (circ) needle size US 4 (3.5 mm)

One 36" (91 cm) circular needle size US 5 (3.75 mm)

One 16" (40 cm) circular needle size US 4 (3.5 mm)

Change needle size if necessary to obtain correct gauge.

GAUGE
20 sts and 28 rows = 4" (10 cm) in Stockinette stitch (St st) using larger needle

19 1/2 sts and 32 rows = 4" (10 cm) in Lace Pattern using smaller needle

NOTIONS
Stitch markers; stitch holders

NOTE
When stitching turned hems on the WS, be careful to catch the part of the st that is closest to the WS surface. This will make the hemline less visible on the RS.

For an explanation of ribbing in different multiples of knit and purl stitches, see page 165.

BODY
Using larger needle and MC, cast on 220 (236, 252) sts. Join for working in the rnd, being careful not to twist sts; place marker (pm) for beginning of rnd and after 110 (118, 126) sts for side seam.

Begin St st; work even for 5 rnds. Purl 1 rnd (fold line).

Establish Ruching: **Continuing in St st, work even for 6 rnds.

Increase Rnd: Kfb into every stitch—440 (472, 504) sts.

Change to smaller needle and St st and work even for 5 rnds.

Decrease Rnd: *K2tog; repeat from * around—220 (236, 252) sts remain. Change to larger needle. Repeat from ** twice.

Change to St st; work even for 3". *NOTE: You may adjust the length of the garment by working more or less than 3" at this point.*

Shape Skirt: Decrease Rnd: *Ssk, knit to 2 sts before marker, k2tog; repeat from * around—216 (232, 248) sts remain. Work even for 5 rnds.

Repeat Decrease Rnd every 6 rnds 10 times—176 (192, 208) sts remain.

Establish Lace Pattern: Change to A and smaller needle; knit 1 rnd.

Begin Lace Pattern. Work entire pattern three times. Knit 1 rnd.

Change to MC and larger needle and work increases as follows:

STITCH PATTERNS

LACE PATTERN

(multiple of 16 sts; 14-rnd repeat)

Rnd 1: *Yo, k6, k2tog; repeat from * around.

Rnds 2, 4, and 6: Knit.

Rnd 3: *K1, yo, ssk, k3, k2tog, yo; repeat from * around.

Rnd 5: *[Yo, ssk] twice, k1, k2tog, yo, k3, yo, ssk, k1, k2tog, yo, k1: repeat from * around.

Rnd 7: *K1, [yo, ssk] twice, k2, yo, sk2p, yo, k2, [k2tog, yo] twice; repeat from * around.

Rnd 8: *K4, yo, ssk, k5, k2tog, yo, k3; repeat from * around.

Rnd 9: *Yo, [k1, yo, ssk] 3 times, k2tog, yo, k1, k2tog, yo, k2tog; repeat from * around.

Rnd 10: *K3, [yo, ssk, k1] twice, k2tog, yo, k1, k2tog, yo, k2; repeat from * around.

Rnd 11: *[K1, yo, ssk] twice, k1, yo, sk2p, yo, [k1, k2tog, yo] twice; repeat from * around.

Rnd 12: *K2, yo, ssk, k1, yo, ssk, k3, [k2tog, yo, k1] twice; repeat from * around.

Rnd 13: *Yo, ssk, k1, yo, ssk, k7, k2tog, yo, k2; repeat from * around.

Rnd 14: *K1, yo, ssk, k11, K2tog, yo; repeat from * around.

Repeat Rnds 1-14 for Lace pattern

Size Small: *M1, knit to 1 st before marker, m1, k1; repeat from * around—180 sts.

Size Medium: Knit 1 rnd—192 sts.

Size Large: *Knit to marker, m1; repeat from * around—210 sts.

Change to 5x1 Rib, as follows: *K5, p1; repeat from * around. Work even for 7 (8, 8)".

Divide for Front and Back: Bind off 5 sts, work in 1x1 Rib to next marker, as follows: * K1, p1; repeat from * to last 0 (0, 1) st, k0 (0, 1)—85 (91, 100) sts remain. Place next 90 (96, 105) sts on holder for Back, dropping markers; turn.

FRONT

Next row (WS): Working on Front sts only, bind off 4 (4, 5) sts, knit the knit sts and purl the purl sts as they face you—81 (87, 95) sts remain.

Shape Armhole: Decrease 1 st at beginning of next 10 rows—71 (77, 85) sts remain. Work even for 2 rows, ending with WS row.

Shape Neck and Shoulders: (RS) Left Side: Work 21 (23, 27) sts, turn, place remaining 50 (54, 58) sts on holder for right side.

Work even for 4", ending with a WS row.

Bind off 7 (8, 9) sts at beginning of next 2 RS rows, then 7 (7, 9) sts at beginning of next RS row.

(RS) Right Side: Join yarn to sts on holder for right side. Bind off center 29 (31, 31) sts, work to end.

Complete as for left side, working shoulder bind-offs on WS rows.

BACK

Join yarn to Back sts on holder. Working in 1x1 Rib as for Front, bind off 5 sts at beginning of row once, then 4 (4, 5) sts once—81, (87, 95) sts remain.

Shape armhole as for Front. Work even for 2", ending with a WS row.

Shape Neck: (RS) Right Side: Work 21 (23, 27) sts, turn, place remaining 50 (54, 58) sts on holder for left side.

Work even for 2", ending with a WS row.

Bind off 7 (8, 9) sts at beginning of next 2 RS rows, then 7 (7, 9) sts at beginning of next RS row.

(RS) Left Side: Join yarn to sts on holder for left side. Bind off center 29, (31, 31) sts, work to end.

Complete as for right side, working shoulder bind-offs on WS rows.

FINISHING

Sew shoulder seams.

Armhole Edging: RS facing, using 16" circ needle, pick up and knit 84 sts evenly spaced around armhole edge. Bind off all sts knitwise.

Fold bottom hem under at fold line and sew to WS, being careful not to let sts show on RS.

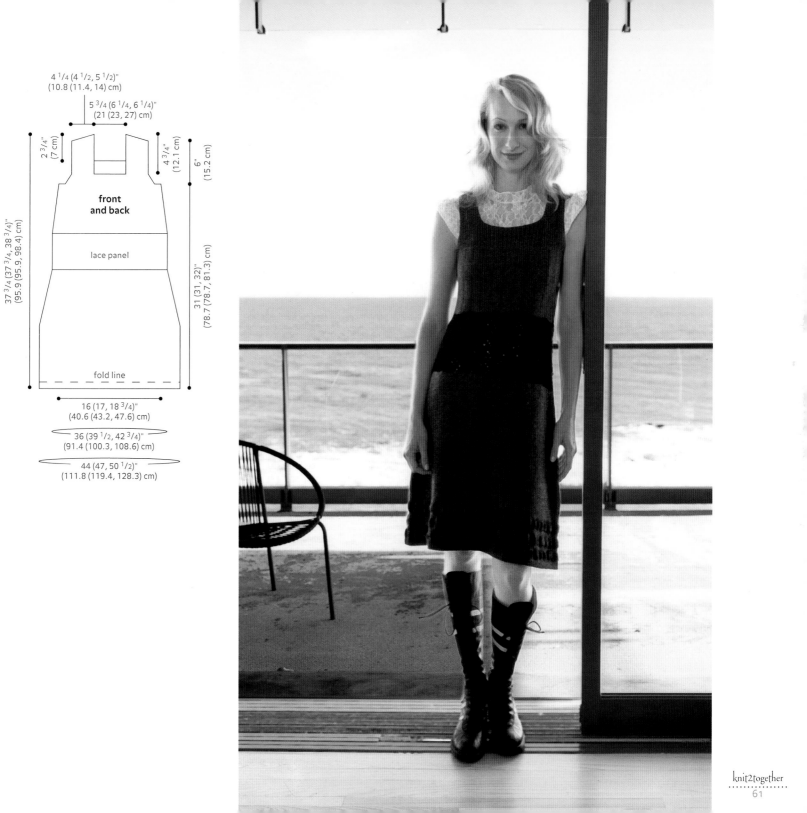

4 1/4 (4 1/2, 5 1/2)"
(10.8 (11.4, 14) cm)

5 3/4 (6 1/4, 6 1/4)"
(21 (23, 27) cm)

2 3/4"
(7 cm)

4 3/4"
(12.1 cm)

6"
(15.2 cm)

**front
and back**

lace panel

37 3/4 (37 3/4, 38 3/4)"
(95.9 (95.9, 98.4) cm)

31 (31, 32)"
(78.7 (78.7, 81.3) cm)

fold line

16 (17, 18 3/4)"
(40.6 (43.2, 47.6) cm)

36 (39 1/2, 42 3/4)"
(91.4 (100.3, 108.6) cm)

44 (47, 50 1/2)"
(111.8 (119.4, 128.3) cm)

WITCHES BRITCHES

These knickers can be worn under the Gym Slip Dress (see page 58) or as sporty, feminine shorts. At my high school we used to wear long underwear like this to keep our thighs warm on winter days. **M**
TRACEY REMEMBERS: *I wish I'd known how to knit these during my school days in freezing cold England. It would have stopped me getting stripy, red thighs from sitting on hot radiators.*

SIZES
To fit 28 (30, 32)" (71.1 (76.2, 81.3) cm) waist

Shown in size 28" (71.1 cm)

FINISHED MEASUREMENTS
28 1/4 (30 1/2, 32)" (71.8 (77.5, 81.3) cm) waist (before adding elastic); 24" (61 cm) long, including finished Waistband and Lace Leg Trim

YARN
Filatura Di Crosa Zara (100% merino wool; 137 yards (125 meters) / 50 grams): 8 balls #1727 granny smith (A), 1 ball #1404 black (B)

NEEDLES
One 24" (60 cm) circular (circ) needle size US 5 (3.75 mm)

One pair straight needles size US 6 (4 mm)

Change needle size if necessary to obtain correct gauge.

NOTIONS
Stitch marker; 1 yard 1" wide elastic

GAUGE
19 sts and 27 rows = 4" (10 cm) in Stockinette st (St st) using larger needles

NOTE
When stitching turned hems on the WS, be careful to catch the part of the st that is closest to the WS surface. This will make the hemline less visible on the RS.

LEFT LEG
Using larger needles and A, cast on 82 (86, 90) sts. Work even in St st for 6 rows, beginning with a knit row.

Shape Leg: (RS) Increase 1 st each side this row, then every 6 rows 9 times—102 (106, 110) sts.

Work even until piece measures 10" or desired length from the beginning, ending with a WS row.

Shape Inside Leg: (RS) Decrease 1 st each side every other row 11 times, then every 4 rows 6 times, ending with a WS row—68 (72, 76) sts remain.

Work even until Leg measures 18" or desired length from the beginning, ending with a WS row.

Shape Rise: (RS) Work short row shaping as follows:

Row 1 (RS): K34 (36, 38), turn.

Row 2: P34 (36, 38), turn.

Row 3: K32 (34, 36), turn.

Row 4: P32 (34, 36), turn.

Row 5: K30 (32, 34), turn.

Row 6: P30 (32, 34), turn.

Row 7: K28 (30, 32), turn.

Row 8: P28 (30, 32), turn

Row 9: K26 (28, 30), turn.

Row 10: P26 (28, 30).

Bind off all sts knitwise.

RIGHT LEG
Work as for Left Leg to beginning of short row shaping. Work even for 1 row.

Row 1 (WS): P34 (36, 38), turn.

Row 2: K34 (36, 38), turn.

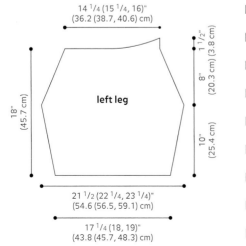

14 1/4 (15 1/4, 16)"
(36.2 (38.7, 40.6) cm)

1 1/2"
(3.8 cm)

8"
(20.3 cm)

18"
(45.7 cm)

left leg

10"
(25.4 cm)

21 1/2 (22 1/4, 23 1/4)"
(54.6 (56.5, 59.1) cm)

17 1/4 (18, 19)"
(43.8 (45.7, 48.3) cm)

Row 3: P32 (34, 36), turn.

Row 4: K32 (34, 36), turn.

Row 5: P30 (32, 34), turn.

Row 6: K30 (32, 34), turn.

Row 7: P28 (30, 32), turn.

Row 8: K28 (30, 32), turn

Row 9: P26 (28, 30), turn.

Row 10: K26 (28, 30).

Bind off all sts purlwise.

FINISHING

Sew Leg seams. Sew center front and back seams. *NOTE: Back seam will be longer than front seam due to extra rows for Rise.*

Waistband: RS facing, using circ needle, and beginning at center back seam, pick up and knit 136 (144, 152) sts around waist. Join for working in the rnd; place marker (pm) for beginning of rnd.

Shape Waistband:

Setup Rnd: [P1, k1] 26 (28, 30) times, p1, k30, [p1, k1] 26 (28, 30) times, p1, m1— 137 (145, 153) sts.

Rnd 1: [P1, k1] 26 (28, 30) times, p1, k30, [p1, k1] 27 (29, 31) times.

Repeat Rnd 1 until Waistband measures 5" from the beginning. Bind off all sts in pattern.

Measure your waist. Cut length of elastic 1" shorter than waist measurement. Sew ends together. Fold top 1" of waistband over elastic to WS and sew in place, being careful not to let sts show on RS.

LACE LEG TRIM

Using smaller needles and B, cast on 9 sts.

Establish Pattern:

Row 1 (RS): K3, [k2tog, yo] twice, k1, yo, k1—10 sts.

Row 2 and all WS Rows: Knit.

Row 3: K2, [k2tog, yo] twice, k3, yo, k1—11 sts.

Row 5: K1, [k2tog, yo] twice, k5, yo, k1—12 sts.

Row 7: K3, [yo, k2tog] twice, k1, k2tog, yo, k2tog—11 sts rem.

Row 9: K4, yo, k2tog, yo, k3tog, yo, k2tog—10 sts rem.

Row 11: K5, yo, k3tog, yo, k2tog—9 sts rem.

Row 12: Knit.

Repeat Rows 1-12 until Trim is long enough to fit around bottom of Leg, ending with Row 12. Bind off all sts. Sew bound-off edge of Trim to cast-on edge. Sew Trim to cast-on edge of Leg, being careful to align Trim seam and inside Leg seam.

If your work needs to measure 12",
put a 12" long string on the end of your needle
so you can measure as you go.

FINISHED MEASUREMENTS
Approximately 12" (30.5 cm) tall

YARN
See page 68.

NEEDLES
One set of four double-pointed needles (dpn) size US 6 (4 mm)

One pair of straight needles size US 3 (3.25 mm)

One 16" (40 cm) circular (circ) needle size US 3 (3.25 mm) for Apron

One pair of straight needles size US 5 (3.75 mm)

One pair of straight needles size US 6 (4 mm)

Change needle size if necessary to obtain correct gauge.

NOTIONS
Stitch markers; stitch holders; fiber filling; two ¹/₂" buttons (Momma Mouse); three ¹/₂" buttons (Art School Mouse); tapestry needle

GAUGE
20 sts and 25 rows = 4" (10 cm) in Stockinette stitch (St st) using largest needles and A

20 sts and 25 rows = 4" (10 cm) in St st using largest needles and 1 strand each of E and F held together

18 sts and 24 rows = 4" (10 cm) in St st using largest needles and G

20 sts and 25 rows = 4" (10 cm) in St st using largest needles and H

20 sts and 25 rows = 4" (10 cm) in St st using largest needles and J

24 sts and 28 rows = 4" (10 cm) in St st using size US 5 needles and K

28 sts and 36 row = 4" (10 cm) in St st using smallest needles and L or M

NOTES
For Short Row Shaping, see Techniques on page 68.

For an explanation of ribbing in different multiples of knit and purl stitches, see page 165.

MEL'S MOUSE FAMILY

I made these cuddly wool-angora mice for my family to remind them of home when they're traveling. My husband loves the beach, so he's the surfer dude shown here. My daughter is a student; my son is an artist and likes to buy his clothes from thrift shops. I like to think of myself as slightly glamorous, even in the kitchen, so Momma Mouse is wearing a cocktail dress and apron. Use this pattern as a template but customize it for your own family. Ⓜ

MOUSE BODY

LEGS (make 2)
Using largest needles and color of your choice (A, B, C, or D), cast on 14 sts. Work even in St st for 34 rows, beginning with a knit row.

Break yarn, leaving 8" tail. *Note: Do not break yarn for second (right) Leg.*

Sew inner Leg seams from cast-on edge halfway up the Leg.

Transfer sts to dpn for left Leg.

JOIN BODY
Using second dpn, work across 14 sts for right Leg, cast on 2 sts, work across 14 sts for left Leg, cast on 2 sts—32 sts. Divide sts evenly among needles as follows: Needle 1: 8 sts; Needle 2: 16 sts for back; Needle 3: 8 sts. Join for working in the rnd; place marker (pm) for beginning of rnd

(this marks the center front of the Body).

Begin St st. Work even for 2 rnds.

Shape Seat:

Work across Needle 1; set aside. Working back and forth on sts on Needle 2, begin Short Row Shaping as follows (see Notes):

Row 1 (RS): K15, wrap next st, turn.

Row 2: P14, wrap next st, turn.

Rows 3-8: Continue as established, working 1 less st each row before wrapping and turning.

Row 9: K8, work wrap together with next st, turn.

Row 10: P9, work wrap together with next st, turn.

Row 11-16: Continue as established, working 1 more st each row before working wrap together with next st.

YARN

Classic Elite Lush (50% angora / 50% wool; 123 yards (112 meters) / 50 grams): 1 hank each #4438 latte (A), #4433 wheat (B), #4416 natural (C), #4475 gray (D)

London Yarns (Needful Yarns) Sinflex (60% tactel / 40% sinflex; 162 yards (150 meters) / 20 grams): 1 ball #118 (E)

Koigu Premium Merino (KPM) (100% merino wool; 175 yards (160 meters) / 50 grams): 1 hank #3010 blue (F)

Cascade Yarns Cascade 220 (100% Peruvian Highland Wool; 220 yards (201 meters) / 100 grams): 1 ball #7804 pink (G)

Filatura di Crosa Zara (100% merino wool; 137 yards (125 meters) / 50 grams): 1 ball #1735 light turquoise (H)

Jaeger Extra Fine Merino DK (100% extra fine merino; 136 yards (124 meters) / 50 grams): 1 ball #978 coal dust (J)

GGH Soft Kid (70% super kid mohair / 25% nylon / 5% wool; 151 yards (138 meters) / 25 grams): 1 ball #74 peach (K)

Koigu Painter's Palette Premium Merino (KPPPM) (100% merino wool; 175 yards (160 meters) / 100 grams): 1 hank #138 (L)

Koigu Premium Merino (KPM) (100% merino wool; 175 yards (160 meters) / 50 grams): 1 hank #2351 (M)

Odd scraps of fingering weight yarn for embroidering facial features (all), Apron detail (Momma Mouse), Surf Shorts detail (Surfer Mouse), Jacket detail (Art School Mouse); lace weight yarn for Scarf (Art School Mouse)

Shown in the following yarns and colors:

Momma Mouse (A), Cocktail Dress (1 strand each of E and F held together), Apron (M); Surfer Mouse (B), Surf Shorts (G); Art School Mouse (D), Jacket (H), Tweed Trousers (J); Vassar Mouse (C), Mohair Sweater (K), Skirt (L)

TECHNIQUES

SHORT ROW SHAPING

Work the number of stitches specified in the instructions, wrap and turn as follows:

Bring yarn to the front (purl position), slip the next st to the right-hand needle, bring yarn to back of work, return slipped stitch on right-hand needle to left-hand needle; turn, ready to work the next row, leaving remaining stitches unworked. *Note: Bring yarn to back if next st to be worked is a knit st.*

When Short rows are completed, work the wrap together with the wrapped st as you come to it as follows:

If stitch is to be worked as a knit st, insert the right-hand needle into the wrap, from below, then into the wrapped st, k2tog; if st to be worked is a purl st, insert needle into the wrapped stitch, then down into the wrap, p2tog. [Wrap may be lifted onto the left-hand needle, then worked together with the wrapped stitch if this is easier.]

Work to end of Needle 2, k1-tbl (first st on Needle 3), work to end of Needle 1, k1-tbl (first st on Needle 2). Work to end of rnd. Work even for 23 rnds.

Shape Neck:

Decrease Rnd:

Needle 1: Work to last 3 sts, k2tog, k1.

Needle 2: K1, ssk, work to last 3 sts, k2tog, k1.

Needle 3: K1, ssk, work to end—28 sts remain.

Knit 1 rnd.

Repeat these 2 rnds twice—20 sts remain.

Knit 1 rnd.

Shape Head:

Increase Rnd:

Needle 1: Work to last 2 sts, kfb, k1.

Needle 2: K1, kfb, work to last 2 sts, kfb, k1.

Needle 3: K1, kfb, work to end—24 sts.

Knit 1 rnd.

Repeat these 2 rnds twice—32 sts.

Knit across Needles 1 and 2; place sts from Needle 2 on holder for back of Head.

Shape Face:

Slip sts from Needle 1 onto end of Needle 3—16 sts. Begin Short Row Shaping as follows (see Notes):

Row 1 (RS): K15, wrap next st, turn.

Row 2: P14, wrap next st, turn.

Rows 3-12: Continue as established, working 1 less st each row before wrapping and turning.

Row 13: K4, work wrap together with next st, turn.

Row 14: P5, work wrap together with next st, turn.

Row 15-24: Continue as established, working 1 more st each row before working wrap together with next st.

Join Head:

Knit across 16 sts on needle; with a new needle, pick up and knit 2 sts from gap between Face and back of Head, knit across 16 sts from holder, pick up and knit 2 sts from gap between back of Head and Face (Needle 1); with a second needle, knit across 8 sts from Face (Needle 2); with a third needle, knit across remaining 8 sts from Face (Needle 3), k1 from Needle 1 onto Needle 3; pm for new beginning of rnd. Slip 1 st from other end of Needle 1 onto Needle 2—18 sts on Needle 1 and 9 sts each on Needles 2 and 3—36 sts.

Shape Top of Head:

Decrease Rnd:

Needle 1: K1, ssk, work to last 3 sts, k2tog, k1.

Needle 2: K1, ssk, work to end

Needle 3: Knit to last 3 sts, k2tog, k1—32 sts remain.

Knit 1 rnd.

Repeat last 2 rnds twice—24 sts remain.

Repeat Decrease Rnd 3 times—12 sts remain.

Slip Needle 2 sts onto Needle 3. Graft sts together using Kitchener st (see page 164). Weave in ends.

FINISHING

Sew cast-on edges of Legs. Fill Body and Head of Mouse. Fill Legs with fiber filling and sew remaining seams.

Embroider nose and eyes with black or dark colored yarn.

EARS (make 2)

Using largest needles and color of your choice (A, B, C, or D), cast on 8 sts.

Row 1 (WS) and all WS rows: Purl.

Row 2: Knit.

Row 4: K1, ssk, k2, k2tog, k1—6 sts remain.

Row 6: K1, ssk, k2tog, k1— 4 sts remain.

Row 8: K1, m1, k2, m1, k1—6 sts.

Row 10: K1, m1, k4, m1, k1—8 sts.

Row 11: Purl.

Bind off all sts.

Fold Ear in half at narrowest point so WS's are together. Sew outside edges. Attach cast-on/bound-off edges to side of Head,

with bound-off edge at the front so that ear curves slight forward (see photo).

ARMS (make 2)

Using largest needles and color of your choice (A, B, C, or D), cast on 11 sts. Work in St st, beginning with a knit row, until piece measures 4" from the beginning.

Shape Arm:

Row 1 (RS): K3, ssk, k1, k2tog, k3—9 sts remain.

Row 2: Purl.

Row 3: K2, ssk, k1, k2tog, k2—7 sts remain.

Break yarn. Thread through remaining sts, pull tight and fasten off. Sew side seam.

Stuff Arm. Sew cast-on edge closed.

Attach cast-on edge of Arm to Body, approximately ³/₄" below narrowest part of neck, with Arm seam facing Body.

TAIL

Using largest needles and color of your choice (A, B, C, or D), cast on 8 sts. Work in St st for 40 rows, beginning with a knit row.

Shape Tail:

Row 1 (RS): K1, ssk, k2, k2tog, k1—6 sts remain.

Rows 2 and 4: Purl.

Row 3: K1, ssk, k2tog, k1—4 sts remain.

Row 5: K1, k2tog, k1—3 sts remain.

Break yarn, thread through remaining sts, pull tight, and fasten off. Do not fill. Sew seam as for Arm.

Attach to Seat.

CLOTHING AND ACCESSORIES

MOMMA MOUSE
COCKTAIL DRESS

Note: Dress is worked in one piece, then sewn together at the back.

Using largest needles and 1 strand each of E and F held together, cast on 54 sts; begin 3x3 Rib, as follows: *K3, p3; repeat from * across. Next row (WS): Knit the knit sts and purl the purl sts as they face you. Work even for 2 more rows (4 rows total).

Next Row (RS): *K1, skp, p3; repeat from * to end—45 sts remain.

(WS) *K1, skp, p2; repeat from * to end—36 sts remain.

Work even in 2x2 Rib as established for 2 rows.

Next Row (RS): K9, pm, k18, pm, k9.

Change to St st, beginning with a purl row. Work even for 17 rows.

Decrease Row (RS): *Work to 2 sts before marker, ssk, slip marker (sm), k2tog; repeat from * once, work to end—32 sts remain.

Work in St st for 13 rows, beginning with a purl row.

Shape Armholes:

Left Back (RS): Work to first marker, turn. Remove marker.

Work even on these 8 sts for 5 rows. Bind off sts knitwise.

Front (RS): Rejoin yarn to remaining 24 sts, work to next marker, turn. Remove marker.

Work even on these 16 sts for 5 rows. Bind off sts knitwise.

Right Back (RS) Rejoin yarn to remaining 8 sts and work as for left back.

Sew 2 sts together at top of each armhole for shoulder. Sew back seam. Weave in ends.

APRON

Using circ needle and M, cast on 12 sts.

Work in St st for 8 rows, beginning with a knit row, increasing 1 st each side this row, then every other row 3 times—20 sts.

Work even for 14 rows, ending with a WS row.

Bind off all sts. Break yarn.

Ruffle: RS facing, using smallest needles and M, pick up and knit 44 sts around 3 edges of Apron (leaving bound-off edge unworked).

Next Row (WS): *Kfb; repeat from * to end—88 sts.

Knit 1 row. Bind off all sts knitwise.

Tie: Using smallest needles and M, cast on 26 sts, pick up and knit 26 sts across top (bound-off edge) of Apron, including side edges of Ruffle, using Knitted Cast-On (see page 164), cast on 26 sts—78 sts.

Bind off all sts. Break yarn. Weave in ends.

Using 2 colors of contrasting scrap yarn, tapestry needle and running st, embroider alternating color stripes across Apron, 1/2" apart.

Sew button to each Ear for earrings.

SURFER MOUSE

SURF SHORTS (make 2)

Note: Each piece forms 1 leg and half the top of the Shorts. The side edges will be sewn together to form the back and front seams from waist to top of legs.

Using largest needles and G, cast on 20 sts. Knit 1 row.

Work in St st for 8 rows, beginning with a knit row.

Shape Shorts: (RS) Increase 1 st each side this row, every 4 rows once, then every other row once—26 sts.

Work even until piece measures 4" from the beginning, ending with a WS row.

Eyelet Row (RS): K2, *yo, k2tog, k1; repeat from * to end.

Purl 1 row.

Change to 1x1 Rib, as follows: *K1, p1; repeat from * across. Next row (WS): Knit the knit sts and purl the purl sts as they face you.

Bind off all sts in pattern.

Sew back and front seam from waist to top of leg, leaving a gap in back seam for Tail. Sew leg seams.

Twisted Cord Tie: Cut one 50" piece of yarn. Make Twisted Cord (see page 165). Thread through Eyelet Row. Embroider flowers (see photo).

ART SCHOOL MOUSE

JACKET

Note: Jacket is worked in 1 piece to armholes, then fronts and back are worked separately to shoulder.

Using largest needles and H, cast on 47 sts. Work in St st for 6 rows, beginning with a knit row.

Buttonhole Row (RS): Work to last 3 sts, yo, k2tog, k1.

Work even for 7 rows, ending with a WS row.

Next Row (RS): K13, k2tog, k17, k2tog, k10, yo, k2tog, k1—45 sts remain.

Work even for 7 rows, ending with a WS row.

Repeat Buttonhole Row. Purl 1 row. Knit 1 row.

Shape Neck and Shoulders:

Left Front: (WS): P13, turn; place remaining 32 sts on holder for back and right front.

Work even for 11 rows.

(WS) Bind off 7 sts purlwise, purl to end—6 sts remain.

Knit 1 row.

(WS) Bind off all sts purlwise.

Back: (WS) Rejoin yarn and purl across 19 sts from holder; leave remaining 13 sts on holder for right front.

Work even for 13 rows.

Bind off all sts knitwise.

Right Front (WS): Rejoin yarn and work across remaining 13 sts from holder.

Work even for 12 rows.

(RS) Bind off 7 sts knitwise, work to end—6 sts remain.

Purl 1 row.

(RS) Bind off all sts knitwise.

SLEEVES (make 2)
Using largest needles and H, cast on 15 sts. Work in St st for 6 rows, beginning with a knit row.

Next Row (RS): Increase 1 st each side this row, then every 4 rows twice—21 sts.

Work even for 7 rows.

Bind off all sts knitwise.

Pinstripes: Using contrasting scrap yarn, tapestry needle and running st, embroider 4 stripes lengthwise on Sleeve, 1/2" apart.

FINISHING
Block all pieces. Sew shoulder seams.

Collar: RS facing, using largest needles and H, pick up and knit 22 sts around neck edge, beginning and ending 1/2" in from each neck edge. Purl 1 row.

Next Row (RS): Knit, increase 1 st each side—24 sts.

Purl 1 row.

Next Row (RS): [Kfb, k4] 4 times, kfb, k2, kfb—30 sts.

Purl 1 row.

Bind off all sts.

Sew Sleeve seams. Sew in Sleeves. Sew buttons opposite buttonholes.

SCARF
Using smallest needles and scrap yarn of your choice, cast on 5 sts; begin Garter st. Work even until Scarf measures 15" from the beginning.

Bind off all sts. Weave in ends.

TWEED TROUSERS
BACK AND FRONT (both alike)
Note: Each piece forms 1 leg and half the top of the Trousers. The pieces will be sewn together to form the back and front seams from waist to top of legs.

Using largest needles and J, cast on 22 sts. Knit 1 row.

Work in St st for 14 rows, beginning with a knit row.

Shape Trousers: (RS) Increase 1 st each side this row, then every 4 rows once—26 sts.

Work even until piece measures 5" from the beginning, ending with a WS row.

Eyelet Row (RS): K2, *yo, k2tog, k1; repeat from * to end.

Purl 1 row.

Change to 1x1 Rib, as follows: *K1, p1; repeat from * across. Next row (WS): Knit the knit sts and purl the purl sts as they face you.

Bind off all sts in pattern.

Sew back and front seam from waist to top of leg, leaving a gap in back seam for Tail. Sew leg seams.

Twisted Cord Tie: Cut one 50" piece of yarn. Make Twisted Cord (see page 165). Thread through Eyelet Row.

VASSAR MOUSE
MOHAIR SWEATER
BACK AND FRONT (both alike)
Using size US 5 needles and K, cast on 27 sts; begin 1x1 Rib, as follows: P1, *k1, p1; repeat from * across. Next row (RS): Knit the knit sts and purl the purl sts as they face you. Work even for 1 more row (3 rows total).

Next Row (RS): Change to St st, beginning with a knit row. Work even until piece measures 4" from the beginning, ending with a WS row.

Change to 1x1 Rib, as follows: K1, *p1, k1; repeat from * across. Next row (WS): Knit the knit sts and purl the purl sts as they face you. Work even for 3 more rows (5 rows total).

Bind off all sts in pattern.

SLEEVES (make 2)
Using size US 5 needles and K, cast on 19 sts; begin 1x1 Rib as for Back. Work even for 3 rows.

Change to St st, beginning with a knit row, increasing 1 st each side every 6 rows twice—23 sts.

Work even until piece measures 2 1/2" from the beginning, ending with a WS row.

Bind off all sts.

FINISHING
Beginning at armhole edge, sew 1" shoulder seams. WS facing, sew side seams, leaving room to sew in Sleeves. Sew Sleeve seams. Sew in Sleeves. Weave in ends.

SKIRT
BACK AND FRONT (both alike)
Using smallest needles and L, cast on 100 sts.

Knit 1 row.

Next Row (RS): K1, *skp; repeat from * to last st, k1—51 sts remain.

Knit 1 row.

Next Row (RS): K13, pm, k25, pm, k13.

Work in St st, beginning with a purl row, decrease 4 sts across next RS row, then every 4 rows 5 times, as follows: *Work to 2 sts before marker, ssk, sm, k2tog; repeat from * once, work to end—27 sts remain.

Purl 1 row.

Change to 1x1 Rib, as follows: K1, *p1, k1; repeat from * across. Next row (WS): Knit the knit sts and purl the purl sts as they face you.

Eyelet Row (RS): *K1, yo, k2tog, p1, repeat from * to last 3 sts, k1, yo, k2tog.

Change to 1x1 Rib as established. Work even for 3 rows.

Bind off all sts in pattern.

FINISHING
Sew side seams.

Twisted Cord Tie: Cut one 50" length of yarn. Make Twisted Cord (see page 165). Thread through Eyelet Row.

DAPHNE'S BABY CAPE

My mother, Daphne, made a simple garter-stitch cape like this one for my daughter, India, when she was born. It's more stylish than a blanket but just as useful for keeping baby warm and snuggly. The loops around the hood are an optional frill. **M** TRACEY SAYS: *Mel insists this cape is suitable for a baby boy too, but I would fear retribution when the lad gets older and sees the photographs. I personally think "The Daphne" is as adorable and girly as it gets.*

SIZES
One size

FINISHED MEASUREMENTS
Approximately 17 1/4" (43.8 cm) x 51" (129.5 cm), not including hood

YARN
Cascade 220 (100% wool; 220 yards (201 meters) / 100 grams): 3 hanks #9407 celery or #9438 Tahiti

NEEDLES
One 36" (91 mm) circular (circ) needle size US 6 (4 mm)

One 24" (60 mm) circular needle size US 3 (3.25 mm)

Change needle size if necessary to obtain correct gauge.

NOTIONS
Stitch markers; stitch holder; four 9/16" buttons

GAUGE
20 1/2 sts and 40 rows = 4" (10 cm) in Garter st using larger needle

NOTES
Techniques: see page 76.

CAPE

Using larger circ needle, cast on 261 sts; begin Garter st. Work even for 2 rows; place removable marker on second st of second row (WS) to mark WS of Cape.

Work even for 23 rows, ending with a RS row.

Shape Cape:

Setup Row: (WS) K18, pm, k1, pm, [k31, pm, k1, pm] 7 times, knit to end.

*Decrease Row (RS): Continuing in Garter st, work to 2 sts before first marker, ssk, sm, k1, sm, k2tog, [work to 2 sts before next marker, ssk, sm, k1, sm, k2tog] 7 times, work to end—245 sts remain.

Work even for 21 rows.

Repeat from * 4 times—181 sts remain after last repeat.

Buttonhole Row (RS): K3, yo, k2tog, work to 2 sts before marker, ssk, sm, k1, sm, k2tog, [work to 2 sts before next marker, ssk, sm, k1, sm, k2tog] 7 times, work to end—165 sts remain. *Note: If you would like to work buttonholes at the left front edge rather than the right front edge, work this row as the Decrease Row above, and work the Buttonhole on the next (WS) row as follows: K3, yo, k2tog, work to end.*

Work even for 3 rows (2 rows if you worked the Buttonhole on a WS row).

(RS) Work Decrease Row—149 sts remain. Work even for 3 rows.

Repeat from * to * once—133 sts remain. Work Buttonhole Row (if working Buttonhole on WS, work even for 1 row, then work Buttonhole Row)—117 sts remain. Work even for 3 rows (2 rows if you worked the Buttonhole on a WS row). **
Repeat from * to ** once—69 sts remain.

MAKE LOOP (ml)

Insert right-hand needle into next st on left-hand needle, [take yarn between 2 needles, then around index finger] twice, then take yarn back between 2 needles again, pulling the 3 loops through st on left-hand and off needle to complete the stitch; yo, slip 3 loops over yo and off needle. *Note: Loops should remain at back of row on which you're working them. To keep loops even, leave them on index finger while you slip loops over yo and off needle.*

Final Buttonhole Row: (RS) K3, yo, k2tog, work to end (if working Buttonhole on WS, work even for 1 row, then work Buttonhole Row). Work even for 3 rows (2 rows if you worked the Buttonhole on a WS row).

Bind off 10 sts at beginning of next 2 rows—49 sts remain.

Work even for 6 rows, ending with a WS row.

Shape Hood Gusset: (RS) Bind off 18 sts at beginning of next 2 rows—13 sts remain.

(RS) Kfb in each st—26 sts.

(WS) Continuing in Garter st, work even until Hood measures 5" from the beginning, ending with a WS row. Break yarn and transfer sts to st holder.

(RS) RS facing, beginning at bottom right edge of Hood Gusset, pick up and knit 24 stitches along right edge, work across 26 sts from holder, pick up and knit 24 sts along left edge of Hood Gusset—74 sts.

Work even in Garter st for 41 rows, ending with a WS row.

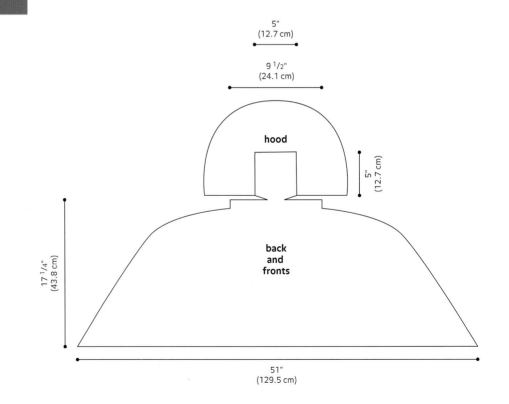

(RS) Change to smaller needle and work even for 8 rows. Bind off all sts.

FINISHING
Sew sides of Hood to bound-off stitches at neck edge, easing Hood edge to gather slightly. Weave in ends. Sew buttons opposite buttonholes.

LOOP TRIM (optional)
Using smaller circ needle, cast on 7 sts; knit 1 row.

Row 1: Sl 1, make loop (ML), [k1, ML] twice, k1.

Row 2: Knit.

Repeat Rows 1 and 2 until piece measures same length as edge of Hood. Bind off all sts. Sew to top of Hood, along front edge.

LACY HUG-ME-TIGHT

This pretty hug-me-tight is inspired by the ones my ancestors wore on their three-month sea voyage from England to New Zealand in the 1850s. Theirs were purely practical, worn for warmth under their jackets. This one, with its pretty lace trim, is flattering as well. This is a very popular project at Wildfiber. It demands concentration but isn't too difficult for a keen beginner. **M**

SIZES
To fit 34-36 (38-40)" (86.4-91.4 (96.5-101.6) cm) bust

Shown in size 34-36" (86.4-91.4 cm)

FINISHED MEASUREMENTS
56 (68)" (142.2 172.7) cm) around cast-on/bound-off edge of Body piece

YARN
Blue Sky Alpacas Alpaca Silk (50% alpaca / 50% silk; 146 yards (133 meters) / 50 grams): 5 balls #i33 blush

NEEDLES
One 29" (74 cm) or 36" (91 cm) circular (circ) needle size US 5 (3.75 mm)

One pair straight needles size US 8 (5 mm)

Change needle size if necessary to obtain correct gauge.

GAUGE
20 sts and 24 rows = 4" (10 cm) in 2x2 Rib, slightly stretched, using smaller needle

NOTES
To work yo before k2tog at beginning of row, insert right-hand needle into first 2 sts, ready to k2tog; bring yarn under needle to the front, then to the back to complete k2tog.

Stitch pattern: see page 80.

BODY
Using smaller needle, cast on 142 (170) sts; begin 2x2 Rib, as follows: P2, *k2, p2; repeat from * across. Next row (WS): Knit the knit sts and purl the purl sts as they face you. Work even until piece measures 21 (24)" from the beginning, ending with a WS row.

Bind off all sts in pattern.

LACE BODY BORDER
Using larger needles, cast on 19 sts. Knit 1 row.

Begin Lace Pattern. Work even until piece measures 60 (72)" from the beginning, ending with Row 12.

Bind off all sts.

LACE ARMHOLE BORDER
Using larger needles, cast on 19 sts. Knit 1 row.

Begin Lace Pattern. Work even until piece measures 12 (14)" from the beginning, ending with Row 12.

Bind off all sts.

FINISHING
NOTE: See diagram for assembly.

Fold Body piece in half so that cast-on and bound-off edges are together. Sew side seams along side edge (not cast-on or bound-off edge), from Hem to 6 (7)" from fold line, leaving armhole opening.

Mark center of cast-on and bound-off edges. Center of cast-on edge will be at back of neck when worn; center of bound-off edge will be above back waist.

Mark center of straight edge of Lace Body Border piece. With RS's of piece facing each other, sew cast-on and bound-off edges of Lace Body Border together.

LACE PATTERN

(panel of 19 sts (at cast-on and bind-off); 12-row repeat)

NOTE: St count changes every RS row.

Row 1 (RS): Slip 1, k2, yo, k2tog, k2, yo, skp, k3, k2tog, yo, k3, yo, k2—20 sts.

Row 2: Yo, k2tog, k15, yo, k2tog, k1.

Row 3: Slip 1, k2, yo, k2tog, k3, yo, skp, k1, k2tog, yo, k5, yo, k2— 21 sts.

Row 4: Yo, k2tog, k16, yo, k2tog, k1.

Row 5: Slip 1, k2, yo, k2tog, k4, yo, sk2p, yo, skp, k2tog, [yo] 3 times, k2tog, k1, yo, k2—22 sts.

Row 6: Yo, k2tog, k3, [k1, p1, k1] into triple yo of previous row, k11, yo, k2tog, k1.

Row 7: Slip 1, k2, yo, k2tog, k2, k2tog, yo, k3, yo, skp, k3, k2tog, yo, k2tog, k1—21 sts remain.

Row 8: Yo, k2tog, k16, yo, k2tog, k1.

Row 9: Slip 1, k2, yo, k2tog, k1, k2tog, yo, k5, yo, skp, k1, k2tog, yo, k2tog, k1—20 sts remain.

Row 10: Yo, k2tog, k15, yo, k2tog, k1.

Row 11: Slip 1, k2, yo, [k2tog] twice, yo, skp, k2tog, [yo] 3 times, k2tog, k1, yo, sk2p, yo, k2tog, k1—19 sts remain.

Row 12: Yo, k2tog, k5, [k1, p1, k1] into triple yo of previous row, k6, yo, k2tog, k1.

With RS's of Lace Border piece and Body piece facing, pin straight edge of Lace Body Border piece at seam to cast-on edge of Body piece at center marker. Pin marked center of Lace Body Border piece to bound-off edge of Body at center marker. Sew pieces together, easing work as necessary to fit.

Sew Lace Armhole Border around armhole openings, beginning and ending at side seam. Weave in all ends.

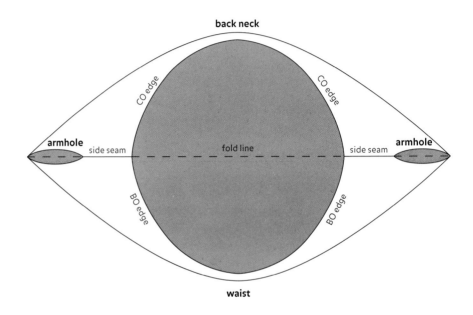

NOTE: The dark gray shaded areas are the WS of the ribbed Body piece.

DOCTOR'S BAG

Here's a bag for your knitting or for stashing pajamas for your next slumber party. Because of its generous size, it can hold all kinds of treasures. The subdued herringbone stitchwork, polished dark wooden handles, and full lining combine to give it a very sophisticated look. Bamboo rods secured into the knitting at the top are the "secret" device that allow it to hold its classic shape. Ⓜ

FINISHED MEASUREMENTS
19 1/2" (49.5 cm) long x 6 3/4" (17.1 cm) wide x 10 1/2" (26.7 cm) high

YARN
Manos del Uruguay Wool (100% wool; 138 yards (126 meters) / 100 grams): 7 hanks #42 marl or #48 cherry

NEEDLES
One pair straight needles size US 11 (8 mm)

Two 24" (60 cm) circular (circ) needles size US 11 (8 mm)

Change needle size if necessary to obtain correct gauge.

NOTIONS
Crochet hook size H/8 (5 mm)

Two 16" bamboo rods or wooden dowels; one pair wooden handles; one 2 1/2" button; one 6x18" plastic or cardboard sheet for base of bag; 1 1/2 yards fabric for lining (optional); removable marker

GAUGE
16 sts and 28 rows = 4" (10 cm) in Herringbone Pattern, using 2 strands of yarn held together

NOTES
Stitch pattern: see page 84.

BACK AND FRONT (both alike)
Using straight needles and 2 strands of yarn held together, cast on 22 sts.

Shape Bag: (RS) Begin Herringbone pattern. Work Rows 1-16 once and, at the same time, cast on 4 sts at beginning of Row 2, every other row 4 times, then every 6 rows once, working cast-on sts in pattern—46 sts after last cast-on.

Work even until piece measures 18" from the beginning, ending with Row 15 of pattern.

Next Row (WS): Continuing in pattern as established, bind off 4 sts at beginning of Row 16, every 6 rows once, then every other row 4 times—22 sts remain.

Work even for 1 row. Bind off all sts in pattern.

SIDES (make 2)
Work as for Back until you have 42 sts (you should have completed Row 10 of pattern).

Work even until piece measures 5 1/4" from the beginning, ending with Row 5.

Next Row (WS): Bind off 4 sts at beginning of this row, then every other row 4 times—22 sts remain.

Work even for 1 row (piece should measure approximately 6 3/4" from the beginning). Bind off all sts in pattern.

BASE
Using straight needles and 2 strands of yarn held together, cast on 78 sts; begin Herringbone pattern.

Work Rows 1-16 three times (piece should measure approximately 6 3/4" from the beginning). Bind off all sts in pattern.

STITCH PATTERN

HERRINGBONE PATTERN

(multiple of 4 sts + 2; 16-row repeat)

Row 1 (RS): K2, *slip 2 wyif, k2; repeat from * to end.

Row 2: P1, *slip 2 wyib, p2; repeat from * to last st, p1.

Row 3: Slip 2 wyif, *k2, slip 2 wyif; repeat from * to end.

Row 4: P3, *slip 2 wyib, p2; repeat from * to last 3 sts, slip 2 wyib, p1.

Row 5-8: Repeat Rows 1-4.

Row 9: Repeat Row 3.

Row 10: Repeat Row 2.

Row 11: Repeat Row 1.

Row 12: Repeat Row 4.

Rows 13-15: Repeat Rows 9-11.

Row 16: Repeat Row 12.

Repeat Rows 1-16 for Herringbone pattern.

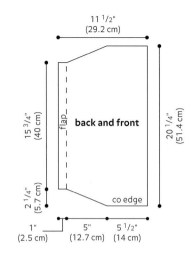

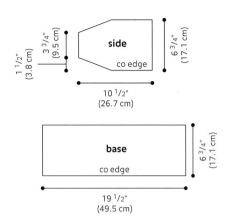

RS facing and using 1/2" seam allowance, sew together Back, Front, Sides and one Base piece (see assembly diagram).

RS facing, sew remaining Base pieces together, leaving one end open. Turn inside out and insert plastic or cardboard sheet; carefully sew Base closed so that seam does not show.

along long edge of Base (AB on assembly diagram). Break yarn. Repeat along straight edge of Front (BA).

WS facing and using 2 strands of yarn held together, join Base to Front using Three-Needle Bind-Off method (see page 165). Repeat for other edge of Base and straight edge of Back.

RS facing and using circ needle and 2 strands of yarn held together, beginning at narrow end of Side, pick up and knit 76 sts as follows: 28 sts along sloped and straight cast-on edge, 20 sts along straight edge, and 28 sts along straight and sloped bound-off edge (EDBC). Break yarn.

OPTIONAL LINING

Lay pieces of Bag on Lining fabric, leaving room to trace 2 additional Base pieces. Trace each Lining piece 1/2" larger than the actual Bag piece. Trace 2 additional Base pieces.

FINISHING

Note: Refer to assembly diagram for assembling Bag.

RS facing and using 2 strands of yarn held together, pick up and knit 60 sts

Leave ends long enough for sewing seams.

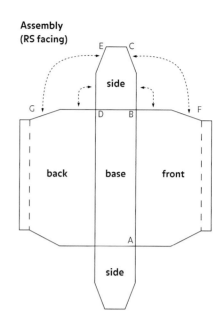

E   C

side

G   D   B   F

back   base   front

A

side

Using second circ needle and 2 strands of yarn held together, beginning 1" in from narrower edge of Front, pick up and knit 76 sts as follows: 28 sts along shaping and cast-on edges of Front, 20 sts along Base, 28 sts along bound-off and shaping edges of Back, ending 1" in from narrower edge of Back (FBDG).

RS facing and using 2 strands of yarn held together, join Side to Bag using Three-

Needle Bind-Off method. Repeat for second Side.

Sew Lining to inside of Bag, being careful not to allow sts to show on outside. Place Lining Base inside Bag. Fold flap (see schematic) over to inside of Bag. Insert bamboo rod under flap and sew flap to Lining (or to Bag if you have no Lining). Sew sides of flap closed to hide rod.

Sew handle to flap on inside of Bag, or

work optional Handle Chains and attach handle to outside of bag as follows:

Handle Chains (optional): Using crochet hook, leaving 8" long tail at beginning and end, work four 3" long crochet chains (see page 164). Thread each Chain through hole in handle, making sure that handle is equidistant from each end of Bag. Secure Chain to Bag around rod using tail.

Button Chain: Using crochet hook, leaving 6" long tail at beginning and end, work one 10" long crochet chain; fasten off. Work ending tail back through Chain, looping Chain back on itself to fit around the button. Mark center of rod on outside Back of Bag; attach other end of Chain to base of rod at marker. Sew button to Front of Bag, so that loop in Chain fits snugly over button.

NEW SCHOOL TIE

This versatile Stockinette-stitch tie—which adapts well to jeans or a business suit—is made with four different colors of hand-dyed yarn. The thin bright orange stripes give your eye a place to rest. I think this tie looks great on men and women. Ⓜ TRACEY NOTES: *I startled Jay Leno by giving him this tie during a* Tonight Show *appearance. I haven't seen him wear it yet, and if I find out he's using it to wipe the windshields on his vintage cars, he can kiss the argyle socks goodbye!*

SIZES
One size

FINISHED MEASUREMENTS
2" (5.1 cm) wide at widest point x 57" (144.8 cm) long

YARN
Koigu Premium Merino (KPM) (100% merino; 175 yards (160 meters) / 50 grams): 1 hank each #2235 wine (A), #2220 bright tangerine (B), #3010 blue gray (C), #2236 dusky grape (D)

NEEDLES
One pair straight needles size US 2 (3 mm)

One set of five 6" double-pointed needles (dpn) size US 2 (3 mm) (optional)

Change needle size if necessary to obtain correct gauge.

NOTIONS
Stitch markers

GAUGE
28 sts and 37 rows = 4" (10 cm) in Stockinette st (St st)

NOTES
Instructions are given for using single-pointed needles, with a seam in the back. However, the Tie looks really good worked in the round on double-pointed needles as well. If you choose to use dpn, the beginning of the rnd will be in the back, and all even-numbered rnds will be knit instead of purl. Be sure to place a marker for beginning of rnd.

The slipped sts create a flat edge along each side of the Tie when it is folded.

TIE
Using straight needles and B, cast on 30 sts.

Establish Pattern:

Row 1 (RS): K7, place marker (pm), k1, pm, k14, pm, k1, pm, k7.

Rows 2 and 4: Purl, slipping all markers.

Row 3: K7, slip marker (sm), slip 1, sm, k14, sm, slip 1, sm, k7.

Repeating Rows 3-4, work stripes as follows: 2 rows B, 18 rows A, 36 rows D, 4 rows C, 16 rows A, 26 rows D, 2 rows B, 6 rows C, 20 rows A, 2 rows B, 14 rows D, 6 rows C.

Shape Tie:

Row 1: (RS) Continuing in C, k5, ssk, sm, slip 1, sm, k2tog, k10, ssk, sm, slip 1, sm, k2tog, k5—26 sts remain.

Rows 2 and 4: Purl, slipping all markers.

Row 3: K6, sm, slip 1, sm, k12, sm, slip 1, sm, k6.

Repeating Rows 3-4, work stripes as follows: 24 rows C [Note: Adjust row count here to lengthen or shorten Tie if desired], 2 rows B, 60 rows A, 2 rows B, 20 rows D, 60 rows C, 12 rows A, 38 rows D, 4 rows B, 12 rows C, 12 rows A, 70 rows D, 2 rows B, 42 rows C, 12 rows A.

Bind off all sts. Fold along slip st edge. Sew center back and end seams. Weave in ends.

SANTA CRUZ HOODIE

This easy sweater can be made for the whole family. It's perfect for a walk on the beach on a chilly day or to throw on after a day of surfing. Ⓜ

SIZES

To fit Child 1 (2, 4, 6, 8-10) years < Adult 36 (38, 40, 42, 44)" (91.4 (96.5, 101.6, 106.7, 111.8) cm) chest>

Shown in size 2 years < 44" (111.8 cm)>

FINISHED MEASUREMENTS

26 (28 1/2, 30, 32 1/2, 34)" (66 (72.4, 76.2, 82.6, 86.4) cm) < 36 1/2 (38, 40 1/2, 42, 43 1/2)" (92.7 (96.5, 102.9, 106.7, 110.5) cm) > chest

YARN

GGH Aspen (50% fine merino wool / 50% microfiber; 62 yards (57 meters) / 50 grams): 10 (10, 11, 11, 12) balls #34, 5 (5, 6, 6, 6) balls #41 <12 (13, 13, 14, 14) balls #25, 5 (6, 6, 6, 6) balls #12 >

NEEDLES

One pair straight needles size US 10 (6 mm)

One pair straight needles size US 11 (8 mm)

One 24" (60 cm) circular (circ) needle size US 10 (6 mm)

Change needle size if necessary to obtain correct gauge.

NOTIONS

Removable markers

GAUGE

12 sts and 16 rows = 4" (10 cm) in Stockinette st (St st) using larger needles

NOTES

Stitch pattern: see page 90.

BACK

Using smaller needles and A, cast on 39 (43, 45, 49, 51) < 55 (57, 61, 63, 65) > sts; begin Seed st. Work even for 5 < 7 > rows.

Establish Pattern:

Child Sizes Only:

Row 1 (RS): K1, p1, knit to last 2 sts, p1, k1.

Row 2: K1, p1, k1, purl to last 3 sts, k1, p1, k1.

Repeat Rows 1 and 2 three times.

Adult Sizes Only:

Row 1 (RS): [K1, p1] twice, knit to last 4 sts, [p1, k1] twice.

Row 2: K1, p1, k1, purl to last 3 sts, k1, p1, k1.

Repeat Rows 1 and 2 three times.

All Sizes:

(RS) Change to larger needles and St st. Beginning with a knit row, work even until piece measures 9 (10, 11, 12, 13)" < 17 (17, 18, 18, 19) " > or desired length from the beginning, ending with a WS row.

Shape Raglan Armhole: (RS) Bind off 2 sts at beginning of next 2 rows—35 (39, 41, 45, 47) < 51 (53, 57, 59, 61) > sts remain.

Decrease 1 st each side this row, then every other row 10 (11, 12, 13, 13) < 15 (15, 17, 18, 18) > times, as follows: K1, ssk, work to last 3 sts, k2tog, k1—13 (15, 15, 17, 19) < 19 (21, 21, 21, 23) > sts remain.

Purl 1 row. Place sts on holder for Back neck.

FRONT

Work as for Back until 9 (10, 11, 12, 12) < 13 (13, 15, 16, 16) > armhole decreases have been completed—17 (19, 19, 21, 23) < 25 (27, 27, 27, 29) > sts remain. Work even for 1 row.

Shape Neck:

Left Side: (RS) K1, ssk, k3 < 5 >; place remaining 11 (13, 13, 15, 17) < 17 (19, 19, 19, 21) > sts on holder for neck, turn work.

(WS) Bind off 1 st at neck edge 2 < 3 > times and, AT THE SAME TIME, decrease 1 st at armhole edge as established 1 < 2 > times—2 sts remain.

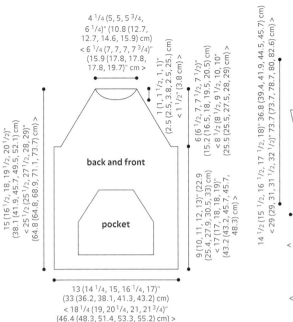

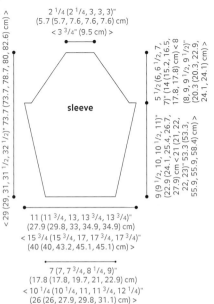

Diagram labels (back and front / pocket):

4 1/4 (5, 5, 5 3/4, 6 1/4)" (10.8 (12.7, 12.7, 14.6, 15.9) cm) < 6 1/4 (7, 7, 7, 7 3/4) (15.9 (17.8, 17.8, 17.8, 19.7)" cm >

1 (1, 1 1/2, 1, 1)" (2.5 (2.5, 3.8, 2.5, 25.) cm) < 1 1/2" (3.8 cm) >

6 (6 1/2, 7, 7 1/2, 7 1/2)" (15.2 (16.5, 18, 19.5, 20.5) cm) < 8 1/2 (8 1/2, 9 1/2, 10, 10" (25.5 (25.5, 27.5, 28, 29) cm) >

15 (16 1/2, 18, 19 1/2, 20 1/2)" (38.1 (41.9, 45.7, 49.5, 52.1) cm) < 25 1/2 (25 1/2, 27 1/2, 28, 29)" (64.8 (64.8, 68.9, 71.1, 73.7) cm) >

9 (10, 11, 12, 13)" (22.9 (25.4, 27.9, 30.5, 33) cm) < 17 (17, 18, 18, 19)" (43.2 (43.2, 45.7, 45.7, 48.3) cm) >

back and front

pocket

13 (14 1/4, 15, 16 1/4, 17)" (33 (36.2, 38.1, 41.3, 43.2) cm) < 18 1/4 (19, 20 1/4, 21, 21 3/4)" (46.4 (48.3, 51.4, 53.3, 55.2) cm) >

Diagram labels (sleeve):

2 1/4 (2 1/4, 3, 3, 3)" (5.7 (5.7, 7.6, 7.6, 7.6) cm) < 3 3/4" (9.5 cm) >

5 1/2 (6, 6 1/2, 7, 7)" (14 (15.2, 16.5, 17.8, 17.8) cm < 8 (8, 9, 9 1/2, 9 1/2)" (20.3 (20.3, 22.9, 24.1, 24.1) cm) >

sleeve

9 1/2 (9 1/2, 10, 10 1/2, 11)" (22.9 (24.1, 25.4, 26.7, 27.9) cm < 21 (21, 22, 22, 23)" 53.3, 55.9, 58.4) cm) >

14 1/2 (15 1/2, 16 1/2, 17 1/2, 18)" 36.8 (39.4, 41.9, 44.5, 45.7) cm) < 29 (29, 31, 31 1/2, 32 1/2)" 73.7 (73.7, 78.7, 80, 82.6) cm) >

11 (11 3/4, 13, 13 3/4, 13 3/4)" (27.9 (29.8, 33, 34.9, 34.9) cm) < 15 3/4 (15 3/4, 17, 17 3/4, 17 3/4)" (40 (40, 43.2, 45.1, 45.1) cm) >

7 (7, 7 3/4, 8 1/4, 9)" (17.8 (17.8, 19.7, 21, 22.9) cm) < 10 1/4 (10 1/4, 11, 11 3/4, 12 1/4)" (26 (26, 27.9, 29.8, 31.1) cm) >

Next Row (RS): Skp—1 st remains. Break yarn, thread through remaining st and fasten off.

Right Side: (RS) Transfer sts from holder to left-hand needle. Rejoin yarn; bind off 5 (7, 7, 9, 11) < 9 (11, 11, 11, 13) > sts, work to last 3 sts, k2tog, k1—5 < 7 > sts remain. Purl 1 row.

(RS) Shape as for left side, working k2tog, k1 at end of row instead of k1, ssk at beginning of row.

SLEEVES

Using smaller needles and B, cast on 21 (21, 23, 25, 27) < 31 (31, 33, 35, 37) > sts; begin Seed st. Work even for 5 < 9 > rows.

Change to larger needles; knit 1 row. Purl 1 row.

Shape Sleeve: (RS) Continuing in St st, increase 1 st each side this row, every 4 rows 5 (6, 7, 7, 6) < 0 > times, then every 8 rows 0 < 7 (7, 8, 8, 7) > times—33 (35, 39, 41, 41) < 47 (47, 51, 53, 53) > sts.

Work even until piece measures 9 (9 1/2, 10, 10 1/2, 11)" < 21 (21, 22, 22, 23)" > or desired length from the beginning, ending with a WS row.

Shape Raglan Armhole: (RS) Bind off 2 sts at beginning of next 2 rows—29 (31, 35, 37, 37) < 43 (43, 47, 49, 49) > sts remain.

Shape raglan as for Back until 7 (7, 9, 9, 9) < 11 > sts remain.

Work even for 1 row. Place sts on holder for neck.

POCKET

Using smaller needles and A, cast on 25 (27, 27, 29, 31) < 32 (34, 36, 38, 38) > sts. Work even in St st, beginning with a knit row, until piece measures 2 1/2 (2 1/2, 3, 4, 4)" < 4 1/2" >, ending with a WS row.

Shape Pocket

Row 1 (RS): K1, p1, ssk, knit to last 4 sts, k2tog, p1, k1—23 (25, 25, 27, 29) < 30 (32, 34, 36, 36) > sts remain.

Row 2: K1, purl to last st, k1.

Repeat Rows 1 and 2 6 (7, 6, 7, 7) < 8 (9, 9, 10, 10) > times—11 (11, 13, 13, 15) < 14 (14, 16, 16, 16) > sts remain. Bind off all sts in pattern.

FINISHING

Sew Sleeves to Front and Back along raglan edges.

Sew Sleeve and side seams, ending side seams at Seed st edging.

Center Pocket on Front of sweater, just above Seed st rows, and stitch in place.

Hood: Place 2 removable markers at center Front neck edge, 1" either side of center front.

RS facing, using smaller circ needles and A, beginning at marker for right neck edge, pick up and knit 5 (5, 5, 6, 6) < 11 > sts to shoulder seam, knit across 7 (7, 9, 9, 9) < 11 > sts from right Sleeve holder, knit across 13 (15, 15, 17, 19) < 19 (21, 21, 21, 23) > sts from Back holder, increasing 13 (15, 11, 11, 11) < 1 > sts evenly spaced across Back sts, knit across 7 (7, 9, 9, 9) < 11 > sts from left Sleeve holder, pick up and knit 5 (5, 5, 6, 6) < 11 > sts to left neck edge marker—50 (54, 54, 58, 60) < 64 (66, 66, 66, 68) > sts.

(WS) Change to larger needles and St st , beginning with a purl row. Work even until piece measures 11 (11 $^{1}/_{2}$, 12, 13, 14)" < 14" > from pick up row, ending with a WS row.

Divide sts evenly between 2 needles (25 (27, 27, 29, 30) < 32 (33, 33, 33, 34) > sts each needle).

Graft sts together using Kitchener st (see page 164). Weave in ends.

Hood Edging: RS facing, using circ needle and A, pick up and knit 63 (67, 69, 75, 81) < 81 > sts around front edge of Hood; DO NOT JOIN. (WS) Begin Seed st. Work even for 4 < 3 > rows.

Bind off all sts in pattern. Sew edges to Front Neck.

SAILOR PANTS

These comfortable pants have wide legs, reminiscent of sailor pants and are knit in a mercerized cotton that drapes beautifully and holds its shape. The triangular coin pocket is decorative, but big enough to hold parking change. **Ⓜ** TRACEY EXPLAINS: *I really wanted to knit sweatpants. Mel pointed out that the knees might bag slightly, but I feel that's part of their charm. This is my daughter modeling them, by the way. I'd recognize that pierced belly button anywhere.*

SIZES
To fit 26 (30, 34)" (66 (76.2, 86.4) cm) waist
Shown in size 30" (76.2 cm)

FINISHED MEASUREMENTS
32 (34 1/2, 36)" (81.3 (87.6, 91.4) cm) hip
37" (94 cm) long, including finished Waistband

YARN
On Line Linie Clip (100% Mako Egyptian cotton; 182 yards (166 meters) / 100 grams): 8 hanks #188 khaki

NEEDLES
One pair straight needles size US 6 (4 mm)
One 32" (80 cm) circular (circ) needle size US 5 (3.75 mm)
Change needle size if necessary to obtain correct gauge.

NOTIONS
Stitch markers; 1 yard 1" elastic

GAUGE
20 sts and 24 rows = 4" (10 cm) in Stockinette stitch (St st) using larger needles

NOTES
If you would like to lengthen or shorten the pants, you may do so in the first 11", before beginning Leg shaping. Be sure to adjust subsequent length measurements appropriately.

LEFT LEG

Using larger needles, cast on 100 (106, 110) sts; begin 1x1 Rib, as follows: *K1, p1; repeat from * across. Next row (WS): Knit the knit sts and purl the purl sts as they face you. Work even for 1".

Next Row (RS): Change to St st, beginning with a knit row. Work even until piece measures 11" or desired length from the beginning, ending with a WS row.

Shape Leg: (RS) Increase 1 st each side this row, then every 6 rows 9 times—120 (126, 130) sts.

Work even until piece measures 22" or desired length from the beginning, ending with a WS row.

Next Row (RS): Decrease 1 st each side this row, every other row 11 times, then every 4 rows 8 times—80 (86, 90) sts remain.

Work even until piece measures 33" or desired length from the beginning, ending with a WS row.

Shape Rise: (RS) Work short row shaping as follows:

Row 1 (RS): K40 (43, 45), turn.

Row 2: P40 (43, 45), turn.

Row 3: K38 (41, 43), turn.

Row 4: P38 (41, 43), turn.

Row 5: K36 (39, 41), turn

Row 6: P36 (39, 41), turn

Row 7: K34 (37, 39), turn

Row 8: P34 (37, 39), turn

Row 9: K32 (35, 37), turn.

Row 10: P32 (35, 37).

Bind off all sts.

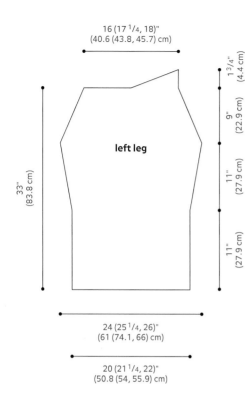

16 (17 1/4, 18)"
(40.6 (43.8, 45.7) cm)

1 3/4"
(4.4 cm)

9"
(22.9 cm)

left leg

11"
(27.9 cm)

33"
(83.8 cm)

11"
(27.9 cm)

24 (25 1/4, 26)"
(61 (74.1, 66) cm)

20 (21 1/4, 22)"
(50.8 (54, 55.9) cm)

RIGHT LEG

Work as for Left Leg to beginning of short row shaping. Work even for 1 row.

Shape Rise: (RS) Work short row shaping as follows:

Row 1 (WS): P40 (43, 45), turn.

Row 2: K40 (43, 45), turn.

Row 3: P38 (41, 43), turn.

Row 4: K38 (41, 43), turn.

Row 5: P36 (39, 41), turn

Row 6: K36 (39, 41), turn.

Row 7: P34 (37, 39), turn

Row 8: K34 (37, 39), turn.

Row 9: P32 (35, 37), turn.

Row 10: K32 (35, 37).

Bind off all sts purlwise.

FINISHING

Sew Leg seams. Sew front and back seams. *NOTE: Back seam will be longer than front seam due to extra rows for Rise.*

Waistband: WS facing, using circ needle and beginning at center back seam, pick up and knit 160 (172, 180) sts around top of Legs. Join for working in the rnd, being careful not to twist sts; place marker (pm) for beginning of rnd.

Rnd 1: [K1, p1] 32 (35, 37) times, k1, p30 (center front), *k1, p1; repeat from * to last st, k1, m1—161 (173, 181) sts.

Rnd 2: [K1, p1] 32 (35, 37) times, k1, p30, *k1, p1; repeat from * around.

Repeat Rnd 2 until Waistband measures 5" from pick-up rnd.

Bind off all sts in pattern.

Measure your waist. Cut length of elastic 1" shorter than waist measurement. Sew ends together. Fold top 1" of waistband over elastic to WS and sew in place, being careful not to let sts show on RS.

Coin Pocket: Cast on 20 sts; begin 1x1 Rib, as follows: *K1, p1; repeat from * across. Next row (WS): Knit the knit sts and purl the purl sts as they face you.

Next Row (RS): Change to St st, beginning with a knit row. Work even for 2 rows.

Shape Pocket: (RS) Decrease 1 st each side this row, then every other row 8 times. Bind off remaining 2 sts.

Sew Pocket to center front of left Leg on RS, beg 1 1/2" below Waistband pick-up row, leaving cast-on edge of Pocket open (see photo).

Why Don't More Men Knit?

So, why, if girls play soccer and join the army, don't more men want to knit? Well, they used to; in fact, they may even have started it all when as hunter-gatherers they knitted nets to catch fish. During the Middle Ages European men formed knitting guilds. It took six years as an apprentice to learn the craft, and to pass their final exams they had to knit a carpet containing flowers, birds, and animals; a beret; a woolen shirt; and, finally, a pair of hose with Spanish clocks, clocks being a fancy heel embellishment not used on commoners' socks. Knitting has not survived as an occupation for men into the present century, and approximately only one man in 20,000 knits as a hobby. But I did hear recently that professional snowboarders have taken to knitting their own hats and wristbands. I can just imagine the conversation in aromatic, smoke-filled cabins the night before a half-pipe event. "Whoa, dude, I just dropped a stitch."

"Hey, dog, get that doobie outta here. You're burning my angora!" T

EVENING BAG

To make this ruffled bag feel right for evening, I used a touch of sparkle in the gathered shimmery sides. The front and back are knit in ribbon. For the handle, I wanted to create something with structure. I had once knitted a necklace with mohair-covered beads, and someone at Wildfiber commented that it would make a perfect bag handle—and so it did. Ⓜ

FINISHED MEASUREMENTS
11" (27.9 cm) wide x 8" (20.3 cm) high

YARN
Crystal Palace Deco Ribbon (70% acrylic / 30% nylon; 80 yards (73 meters) / 50 grams): 1 ball #103 blue/black (A)

Rowan Lurex Shimmer (80% viscose / 20% polyester; 103 yards (94 meters) / 25 grams): 4 balls #339 midnight (B)

Rowan Kid Silk Haze (70% super kid mohair / 30% silk; 229 yards (209 meters) / 25 grams): 1 ball #593 lord (C)

NEEDLES
One pair straight needles size US 10½ (6.5 mm)

One 24" (60 cm) circular (circ) needle size US 6 (4 mm)

One pair double-pointed needles (dpn) size US 3 (3.25 mm)

Change needle size if necessary to obtain correct gauge.

NOTIONS
Tapestry needle; ¼ yard satin; ¼ yard polyester batting (or foam padding); nine ⁹/₁₆" oval wooden beads; two ½" rhinestone buttons or beads; sewing needle and thread to match B.

GAUGE
20 sts and 24 rows = 4" (10 cm) in Stockinette st (St st) using size US 6 needle and 2 strands of B held together

14 sts and 21½ rows = 4" (10 cm) in St st using largest (size US 10½) needles and A

BACK AND FRONT (both alike)
Using largest needles and A, cast on 26 sts. Work in St st for 6 rows, beginning with a knit row, increasing 1 st each side on second and third RS rows—30 sts. Work even for 20 rows.

Shape Bag: (RS) Continuing in St st, decrease 1 st each side this row, every other row 3 times, then every row 4 times—14 sts remain. Bind off all sts.

Using Front as template, cut 2 pieces of lining fabric ½" larger than Front. Cut 2 pieces of batting to exact size of Front. Set aside for Finishing.

RUCHING
RS facing, using size US 6 needle and 2 strands of B held together, pick up and knit 92 sts around shaping edge of Front; begin St st, beginning with a purl row.

Shape Ruching: (RS) *Kfb; repeat from * across—184 sts. Continuing in St st, beginning with a purl row, work even for 5 rows.

Begin Short Row Shaping (RS): K124, turn, p64, turn, k76, turn, p88, turn, k100, turn, p112, turn, k124, turn, p124, turn, k112, turn, p100, turn, k88, turn, p76, turn, k64, turn, p124.

(RS) Work even on all sts for 4 rows.

(RS) *K2tog; repeat from * across—92 sts remain.

Purl 1 row. Bind off all sts.

Optional: Using Ruching as template, cut piece of lining fabric ½" larger than Ruching. Set aside for Finishing.

FINISHING
Sew shaping edge of Back to bind-off edge of Ruching. The cast-on edges of Back and Front form the Bag opening, and the Ruching forms the bottom and sides.

A Close Call

I was in London recently, being driven home in the early hours of the morning, after a long night of filming. I was bleary-eyed and really not capable of knitting, but I was very keen to finish a gorgeous cardigan designed by Patricia Roberts. I had already been working on this cardigan for months. It was in a fine navy blue cotton with contrasting striped pockets in buttercup and sage angora on size 2 needles—had the needles been any smaller, I would have been knitting on cocktail sticks. It was dark in the back of the car, but I was so used to the stitch pattern at this point that I could do it with my eyes closed, which they very nearly were.

I arrived at my house and packed up my knitting bag. "Sleep well, Tracey," said my driver, Terry, as I fumbled with my front-door key and he drove away. Then I began to feel a strange tugging sensation at my hip. I looked down and, in the early dawn light, I could see a strand of yarn reaching down to the ground, over my front step, and out into the road. The strand was getting longer and longer as Terry increased his speed. I let out a scream. "My yarn!" Suddenly, my needles and knitting jumped from the bag and began to bounce across the road. "Terry! Stop! Oh, for God's sake, please stop!!" The tiny needles glinted in the light as they bounced through puddles and the remains

of a Chinese meal spilt from its carton. I was fully awake now, screaming, flapping my arms, and running after the car, which was gaining speed. A passerby, seeing me so distressed, stubbed out his cigarette and joined in my cries for help. "Don't worry, Love, we'll stop him," he reassured me. Luckily, at that moment a garbage truck blocked the main junction and I saw Terry slow to a halt. I ran alongside the car, puffing and panting, and banged on his window. "Terry, please. My knitting . . . it's trapped!" My neighbors had woken up by now and were looking out of their windows to see what all the commotion was about. Apologizing profusely, Terry opened the back door and I retrieved the mother ball. The helpful passerby was surprised to see not an abducted baby, but a ball of blue yarn.

I walked back to the dragging victim and picked it up, brushing off water and noodles. "It's okay!" I shouted to the onlookers. "Only 8 stitches dropped and after a dip in some warm soap and water, this one is going to be just fine!"

I thought I heard mumblings of "bloody actresses" and "talk about a drama queen" as they closed their windows and went back to bed.

But I didn't care. I had averted a disaster. **T**

Handle: Using dpn and 2 strands of C held together, cast on 12 sts; begin St st. Work even for 15". Bind off all sts.

Fold piece in half lengthwise. Sew side seam and one end seam. Insert beads inside piece, end to end. *Note: Beads will be hidden inside Handle, but wrapping them on the outside as follows will add strength and shape to the Handle.* Using tapestry needle and single strand of B, wind yarn around piece several times, between first and second beads; secure yarn. *Thread needle through next bead; wind yarn around piece several times; secure yarn. Repeat from * until one bead remains. Fasten off and weave in end.

Lining: WS of Bag facing, fold Lining pieces over batting and, using $1/2$" seam allowance, sew Lining pieces to Front, Back, and Ruching (optional).

Loops: Using dpn and single strand of B, cast on 3 sts; work I-cord (see page 164) $1 1/2$" long. Work 3 more the same length, two $3 1/2$", and two 5" long. Sew one $1 1/2$" I-cord to each end of cast-on edge of Front and Back, securing both ends of each piece to edge of Bag to form a loop. Thread one $3 1/2$" I-cord through each of the two loops on one end, making a chain; using sewing needle and thread, sew ends together. Repeat for other end. Sew Handle to center link of chain at each end of Bag.

Ties: Sew 5" I-cord at center Front and Back edge of opening. Sew button or bead to end of each.

Never knit a lace pattern or anything complicated when you're tired.

TUTU TEA COZY

Tracey and I take our tea very seriously, so a tea cozy is essential. Your tea will stay piping hot in this outfit made with sparkly fluffy wool-angora mix yarn and mohair tutu frills. Ⓜ

SIZE
To fit a teapot with 16-20" (40.6–50.8 cm) circumference

FINISHED MEASUREMENTS
22 ¹/₂" (57.2 cm) circumference at cast-on edge

YARN
Rowan Yarn Classic Soft Lux (64% extra fine merino / 24% nylon / 10% angora / 2% metallic fiber; 137 yards (125 meters) / 50 grams): 1 ball #04 ciel (A)

GGH Soft Kid (70% super kid mohair / 25% nylon / 5% wool; 151 yards / 25 grams): 1 ball #72 pastel blue (B)

NEEDLES
One pair straight needles size US 6 (4 mm)

One pair straight needles size US 7 (4.5 mm)

One pair double-pointed needles (dpn) size US 6 (4 mm)

NOTIONS
Stitch markers; stitch holders

GAUGE
16 sts and 20 rows = 4" (10 cm) in Stockinette stitch (St st) using larger needles and A

20 sts and 25 rows = 4" (10 cm) in St st using larger needles and B

BODY

Using smaller straight needles and A, cast on 90 sts; begin Garter st. Work even for 5 rows.

Next Row (WS): Change to larger needles. K3, purl to last 3 sts, k3. Knit 1 row. Work even as established until piece measures 2" from the beginning, ending with a RS row.

Next Row (WS): K3, p39, k6, p39, k3.

(RS) K45, turn; place remaining 45 sts on holder for left side.

Right Side Spout Opening

Row 1: (WS): K3, p39, k3.

Row 2: K16, place marker (pm), k13, pm, k16.

Rows 3, 5, and 7: K3, p39, k3, slipping markers.

Rows 4, and 6: K16, sm, k13, sm, k16.

Row 8: *Knit to 2 sts before marker, k2tog, sm, ssk; repeat from * once, knit to end—41 sts remain.

Rows 9 and 11: K3, purl to last 3 sts, k3.

Row 10: Knit.

Rows 12-15: Repeat Rows 8-11—37 sts remain.

Break yarn; place sts on holder, leaving markers in place.

Left Side Spout Opening

Rejoin yarn to sts on holder. Knit 1 row. Work as for right side from Row 1. Do not break yarn.

Join Sides: Working across all 74 sts,

Row 1 (RS): *Knit to 2 sts before marker, k2tog, sm, ssk; repeat from * 3 times, knit to end—66 sts remain.

Row 2: K3, p27, k6, p27, k3, slipping markers.

Row 3: Knit.

Row 4: K3, purl to last 3 sts, k3.

Row 5: Repeat Row 1—58 sts remain.

Row 6: K3, purl to last 3 sts, k3.

Bind off all sts.

TIE

Using dpn and A, cast on 2 sts; work I-cord (see page 164) 32" long. Fasten off. Set aside.

RUFFLE 1

Using larger needles and B, cast on 250 sts. Work in St st for 4 rows, beginning with a knit row.

Next Row (RS): *K2tog; repeat from * to end—125 sts remain.

Purl 1 row.

Bind off all sts.

RUFFLE 2 (make 2)

Using larger needles and B, cast on 120 sts.

Work as for Ruffle 1—60 sts remain.

RUFFLE 3 (make 2)

Using larger needles and B, cast on 90 sts.

Work as for Ruffle 1—45 sts remain.

RUFFLE 4

Using larger needles and B, cast on 140 sts.

Work as for Ruffle 1—70 sts remain.

FINISHING

Sew Ruffle 1 around lower edge, 1 1/2" above cast-on edge.

Sew one Ruffle 2 on each side, from handle edge to spout hole, 1 1/2" above Ruffle 1.

Sew each Ruffle 3 as for Ruffle 2, 1 1/2" above Ruffle 2.

Sew Ruffle 4 to bound-off edge.

Measure 10" in from either end of Tie; place markers. Sew Tie to bound-off edge of Body and Ruffle 4, between markers.

Insert the teapot spout into the Spout Opening and tie the Tie just above the teapot handle.

If you've made one sock and you're not sure if you have enough yarn for its partner, weigh the sock on a kitchen scale, then weigh the remaining yarn.

What's Knit and What's Knot

KNIT	KNOT
Patience	Knitting under the influence
Checking your gauge	Blaming the pattern when you didn't follow the instructions
Fixing your own mistakes	Knots
Teaching a friend	Treating knitting like an extreme sport
Knitting because you love it	Knitting because it's trendy

BUTTERFLY PULLOVER

Here's a henley-style tunic with a stylized butterfly to remind you of summer days. For the butterfly, I adapted an image I found in a book of Chinese motifs. The chinoiserie-style flower comes from a traditional Chinese blockprint. **M**

SIZES
To fit 34-36 (38, 40, 42)" (86.4-91.4 (96.5, 101.6, 106.7) cm) chest
Shown in size 38" (101.6 cm)

FINISHED MEASUREMENTS
43 (45 1/2, 47 1/2, 49 1/2)" (109.2 (115.6, 120.7, 125.7) cm) chest

YARN
Filtes King Koala (64% wool / 28% acrylic / 8% alpaca; 95 yards (86.9 meters) / 50 grams): 10 (11, 12, 12) balls #116 (MC); 1 ball each #15 (A), #165 (B), and #703 (C).

NEEDLES
One pair straight needles size US 7 (4.5 mm)

One pair straight needles size US 8 (5 mm)

One 24" (60 cm) circular (circ) needle size US 7 (4.5 mm)

Change needle size if necessary to obtain correct gauge.

NOTIONS
Stitch markers; 2 stitch holders; two 3/4" buttons

GAUGE
15 sts and 21 rows = 4" (10 cm) in Stockinette stitch (St st) using larger needles

NOTES
Stitch pattern: see page 106.

Charts are read from right to left for RS rows, and from left to right for WS rows; the Charts all begin on RS rows.

FRONT

Using smaller needles and MC, cast on 81 (85, 89, 93) sts; begin Seed st. Work even for 8 rows, ending with a WS row.

(RS) Change to larger needles and St st, beginning with a knit row, keeping first and last 3 sts in Seed st as established. Work even for 2 rows.

Work Butterfly:

Row 1 (RS): Work in Seed st as established for 3 sts, k42 (46, 50, 54), place marker (pm), work 31 sts from Chart A, pm, k2, work in Seed st as established to end.

Row 2: Work in Seed st for 3 sts, p2, slip marker (sm), work 31 sts from Chart, sm, p42 (46, 50, 54) sts, work in Seed st to end. Work even for 2 (4, 4, 4) more rows.

(RS) Continue in St st, omitting Seed st edges, and continuing to work Chart between markers.

Work even until entire Chart is complete, ending with a WS row.

(RS) Continuing in MC, work even in St st, beginning with a knit row, removing markers, for 4 (10, 16, 20) rows, ending with a WS row.

Work Flower: (RS) Continuing in St st, work 6 (8, 10, 12) sts, pm, work 27 sts from Chart B, pm, work to end.

Work even as established until Row 24 of Chart has been completed.

Shape Armhole: (RS) Continuing in St st and working Chart as established, bind off 4 sts at beginning of next 2 rows—73 (77, 81, 85) sts remain.

Decrease 1 st each side every row 6 (8, 10, 12) times, and AT THE SAME TIME, beginning on Row 7 of armhole shaping,

Shape Left Placket Opening and Neck: (RS) Work to marker, sm, k5, place remaining 35 (37, 39, 41) sts on holder for right side, turn, work to end.

Continuing with armhole shaping and Chart, work even until Row 45 of Chart has

back and front

7 1/2" (19.1 cm)

4 1/4" (10.8 cm)

1 1/4" (3.2 cm)

2 3/4" (7 cm)

1" (2.5 cm)

3 3/4 (4 1/4, 4 3/4, 5 1/4)" (9.5 (10.8, 12.1, 13.3) cm)

7 1/2 (8, 8 1/2, 9)" (19.1 (20.3, 21.6, 22.9) cm)

24 (25 1/2, 27 1/4, 28 1/2)" (61 (64.8, 69.2, 72.4) cm)

16 1/2 (17 1/2, 18 3/4, 19 1/2)" (41.9 (44.5, 47.6, 49.5) cm)

21 1/2 (22 3/4, 23 3/4, 24 3/4)" 54.6 (57.8, 60.3, 62.4) cm)

sleeve

15 (16, 17, 18 1/4)" (38.1 (40.6, 43.2, 46.4) cm)

2 3/4 (3 1/4, 3 1/2, 4)" (7 (8.3, 8.9, 10.2) cm)

21 3/4 (22 1/4, 22 1/2, 23)" (55.2 (56.5, 57.2, 58.4) cm)

19" (48.26 cm)

10 3/4 (11 1/4, 11 3/4, 12 1/4)" (27.3 (28.6, 29.8, 31.1) cm)

been completed, ending with a RS row—28 sts remain.

(WS) Bind off 5 sts, work to end—23 sts remain.

(RS) Decrease 1 st at neck edge every row 4 times—19 sts remain.

(RS) Continuing in MC, decrease 1 st at neck edge every row 3 times—16 sts remain.

Work even until armhole measures 7 1/2 (8, 8 1/2, 9)", ending with a WS row.

Shape Shoulder: (RS) Bind off 8 sts at armhole edge twice.

Shape Right Placket Opening, Neck, and Shoulders: RS facing, using MC, rejoin yarn at neck edge. Continuing armhole shaping as established, bind off 5 sts, work to end—29 (31, 33, 35) sts remain. Complete as for left side, reversing all shaping.

BACK

Work as for Front, omitting Charts A and B, until 10 rows of armhole shaping have been completed, ending with a WS row; pm on either side of center 25 sts.

Work Flower: (RS) Work to first marker, slip marker (sm), work 25 sts from Chart C, sm, work to end.

Continuing armhole shaping and Chart as established, work even until entire Chart

is complete, ending with a RS row—61 sts remain.

(WS) Continuing in MC, work even until armhole measures 7 1/2 (8, 8 1/2, 9)", ending with a WS row.

Shape Shoulders and Neck: (RS) Bind off 8 sts, work 8 sts, turn; p2tog, work to end. Bind off 8 sts. Break yarn.

(RS) Rejoin yarn to remaining sts, work to end. Bind off 8 sts, work 8 sts, turn; k2tog, work to end. Bind off 8 sts. Break yarn.

Rejoin yarn to remaining 27 sts. Bind off all sts.

SLEEVE (make 2)

Using smaller needles and MC, cast on 40 (42, 44, 46) sts; begin Seed st. Work even for 15 rows.

(WS) Change to larger needles and St st, beginning with a purl row. Work even until piece measures 7" from the beginning, ending with a WS row.

Shape Sleeve: (RS) Increase 1 st each side this row, every 4 rows 0 (0, 0, 3) times, every 6 rows 2 (6, 9, 7) times, then every 8 rows 5 (2, 0, 0) times—56 (60, 64, 68) sts.

Work even until piece measures 19" from the beginning, ending with a WS row.

Shape Cap: (RS) Bind off 4 sts at beginning of next 2 rows—48 (52, 56, 60) sts remain.

Decrease 1 st each side every row 13 (15, 17, 19) times—22 sts remain. Bind off all sts.

FINISHING

Sew shoulder seams.

Button Placket: Using smaller needles and MC, cast on 5 sts; begin Seed st as follows: All Rows: [P1, k1] twice, p1. Work even for 15 rows; place sts on holder for Neckband.

Buttonhole Placket: RS facing, using smaller needles and MC, pick up and knit 5 sts at center Front neck edge.

(WS) Begin Seed st as for Button Placket. Work even for 7 rows.

Buttonhole Row: P1, k1, yo, k2tog, p1. Work even for 7 rows. Do not break yarn; place sts on holder for Neckband.

Stitch Buttonhole Placket to right Placket Opening. Stitch cast-on edge of Button Placket to pick-up edge of Buttonhole Placket, on WS. Stitch Button Placket to left Placket Opening.

Neckband: RS facing, using yarn attached to Buttonhole Placket and circ needle, work in Seed st across 5 sts from Buttonhole Placket holder, pick up and knit 20 (22, 24, 26) sts along right front neck edge, 25 sts across back neck edge, and 20 (22, 24, 26) sts along left front neck

edge, work in Seed st across 5 sts from Button Placket holder—75 (79, 83, 87) sts.

(WS) Working back and forth on needle, begin Seed st as follows: *P1, k1; repeat from * to last st, p1. Repeat last row twice.

Buttonhole Row: (RS) P1, k1, yo, k2tog, p1, work to end. Work even for 3 rows. Bind off all sts in pattern.

Sew Sleeve and side seams, ending side seams at Seed st edging. Sew in Sleeves.

KEY

- ☐ St st – knit on RS, purl on WS.
- ☐ MC
- ☐ A
- ☐ B
- ☐ C

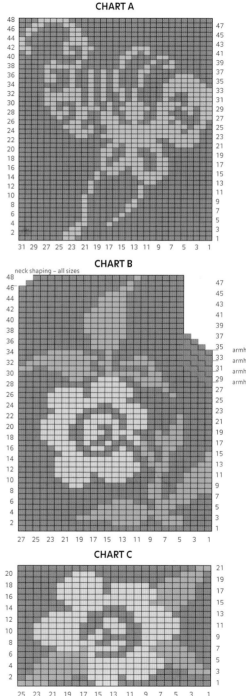

CHART A

CHART B

neck shaping – all sizes

armhole shaping size 42
armhole shaping size 40
armhole shaping size 38
armhole shaping size 34–36

CHART C

PIMLICO SHRUG

I named this after the neighborhood in London where my son attended art school. English girls have a way of wearing a big, sloppy cardigan over a dress or jeans and making it look stylish. A cross between a cardigan and a shawl, this cozy shrug is flattering for all shapes and sizes. It's knit in a large eyelet pattern with a flared edging that makes a dramatic collar. **M** TRACEY: *I loved knitting this shrug. The eyelet stitch needs some extra concentration but is easy once you get going, and the fan collar fools you into thinking you have a neck like Audrey Hepburn's.*

SIZES
Small-Medium (Medium-Large)
To fit 32-36 (36-42)" (81.3-91.4 (91.4-106.7) cm) chest
Shown in size Small-Medium

FINISHED MEASUREMENTS
68 (71)" (172.7 (180.3) cm) around cast-on/bound-off edge of Body piece

YARN
Koigu Kersti (100% merino wool; 114 yards (104 meters) / 50 grams): 14 hanks #1305

NEEDLES
One 47" (120 cm) circular (circ) needle size US 7 (4.5 mm)

One 36" (90 cm) circular needle size US 8 (5 mm)

One set of five double-pointed needles (dpn) size US 7 (4.5 mm)

Change needle size if necessary to obtain correct gauge.

NOTIONS
Stitch marker

GAUGE
19 sts and 25 1/2 rows = 4" (10 cm) in Eyelet Stitch using larger needles

NOTES
Stitch pattern and techniques: see page 110.

BODY
Using larger needles, cast on 161 (169) sts; begin Eyelet st.

Work even until piece measures approximately 34" from the beginning, ending with Row 11 of pattern.

Bind off all sts.

SLEEVES
Using dpn, cast on 52 (56) sts. Divide sts evenly among needles. Join for working in the rnd, being careful not to twist sts; place marker for beginning of rnd. Begin 2x2 Rib, as follows: K2, p2; repeat from * around.

Work even until piece measures 7 1/2" from the beginning.

Next Rnd: *K1, m1, k1, p1, m1p, p1; repeat from * around—78 (84) sts.

Continuing in 3x3 Rib as established, work even until piece measures 10 1/2" from the beginning.

Bind off all sts in pattern.

FINISHING
Note: See diagram for assembly.

Fold Body piece in half so that cast-on and bound-off edges are together. Sew side seams along side edge, from cast-on/bound-off edges to 5 (5 1/2)" from fold line, leaving armhole opening unsewn.

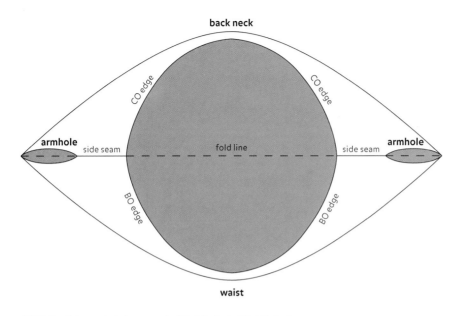

NOTE: The dark gray shaded areas are the WS of the Eyelet Stitch Body piece.

EDGING

RS facing, using smaller circ needle, pick up and knit 320 (336) sts around cast-on and bound-off edges of Shrug. Join for working in the rnd, place marker for beginning of rnd. Begin 2x2 Rib as for Sleeves.

Work even until piece measures 2 1/2" from pick-up rnd.

Next Rnd: *K1, m1, k1, p1, m1p, p1; repeat from * around—480 (504) sts.

Continuing in 3x3 Rib as established, work even for 3".

Bind off all sts in pattern.

Sew Sleeves into armholes. Weave in ends.

STITCH PATTERN/TECHNIQUES

K1B

Knit into back of st in row below next st on left-hand needle, inserting right-hand needle into st from the top down.

K1B-F

Knit into front of st in row below next st on left-hand needle.

K3-S

Knit together 3 loose strands from dropped yo's of previous rows, inserting right-hand needle under loose strands from front to back.

EYELET STITCH

(multiple of 8 sts + 9; 16-row repeat)

Note: St count varies. Original st count is restored on Rows 6, 7, 8, 14, 15, and 16.

*When binding off sts in Eyelet St pattern, k1, *k1, bind off 1 st; repeat from * twice.*

Rows 1 and 3 (WS): Purl.

Row 2: Knit.

Row 4: K3, *bind off 3 sts, k4; repeat from * to last 6 sts, bind off 3 sts, k2.

Row 5: P3, *yo, p5; repeat from * to last 3 sts, yo, p3.

Row 6: K2, *[k1b, k1] in 1 st, yo, drop yo of previous row, [k1b-f, k1] in 1 st, k3; repeat from * to last 5 sts, [k1b, k1] in 1 st, yo, drop yo of previous row, [k1b-f, k1] in 1 st, k2.

Row 7: P4, *yo, drop yo of previous row, p7; repeat from * to last 5 sts, yo, drop yo of previous row p4.

Row 8: K4, *drop yo of previous row, k3-s, k7; repeat from * to last 5 sts, drop yo of previous row, k3-s, k4.

Rows 9 and 11: Purl.

Row 10: Knit.

Row 12: K7, *bind off 3 sts, k4; repeat from * to last 2 sts, k2.

Row 13: P7, *yo, p5: repeat from * to last 2 sts, p2.

Row 14: K6, *[k1b, k1] in 1 st, yo, drop yo of previous row, [k1b-f, k1] in 1 st, k3; repeat from * to last 3 sts, k3.

Row 15: P8, *yo, drop yo of previous row, p7; repeat from * to last st, p1.

Row 16: K8, *drop yo of previous row, k3-s, k7; repeat from * to last st, k1.

Repeat Rows 1-16 for Eyelet Stitch.

YARN
**Koigu Premium Merino (KPM)
(100% merino wool; 175 yards
(160 meters) / 50 grams): 5 hanks
#1300 brown (MC); 1 hank each
#1113 melon (A), #1145 hot coral
(B), #2343 light olive (C), #2300 sky
blue (D), #3010 peacock (E), #1013
lilac (F), #2335 chartreuse (G),
#2166 denim (H)**

NEEDLES
**One pair straight needles size
US 2 (3 mm)**

**One pair straight needles size
US 3 (3.25 mm)**

**One 16" (40 cm) circular (circ)
needles size US 2 (3 mm)**

**Change needle size if necessary to
obtain correct gauge.**

NOTIONS
Removable marker; stitch markers

GAUGE
**30 sts and 33 rows = 4" (10 cm) in
Fair Isle pattern from Chart using
larger needles**

**24 sts and 48 rows = 4" (10 cm) in
Garter st using larger needles**

NOTES
**The Vest is asymmetrical. The Front
and Back have left armhole shaping
only. The Gusset, which is sewn
to the Front and Back along their
straight edges, has right armhole
shaping only. After working the
ribbing, the Front and Back are
both worked from the Chart,
beginning and ending as indicated.
You may work armhole and neck
shaping from the Chart, or as given
in the text.**

TROPICAL GARDEN VEST

*I think of this as a classic grandfather's Fair Isle vest deconstructed.
I have always loved Fair Isle patterns and wanted to invent my own.
The motifs here are inspired by South American textiles, with birds
and butterflies giving a hint of the tropics. At one side a garter stitch
panel is worked as a separate piece and wrapped around from front
to back, in this case with a little swing added to the drape by working
short rows at the hem. Leave out the side panel and make it entirely
in the Fair Isle pattern if you'd like.* Ⓜ

BACK
Using smaller needles and MC, cast on
106 sts; begin 1x1 Rib, as follows: *K1, p1;
repeat from * across. Next row (WS): Knit
the knit sts and purl the purl sts as they face
you. Work even until piece measures 2 1/2"
from the beginning, ending with a WS row.

Next Row (RS): Change to larger needles
and Fair Isle Chart, beginning and ending
as indicated in Chart. Work even through
Row 90 of Chart.

Shape Armhole: (WS) Continuing to work
Chart as established, bind off 6 sts at
armhole edge once, then 1 st every row
12 times—88 sts remain.

Work even through Row 152 of Chart.

Shape Neck: (RS) Work 14 sts, turn; place
remaining 74 sts on holder for neck and
left side.

Right Side: (WS) Decrease 1 st at neck edge
every row 3 times—11 sts remain. Bind off
all sts.

Neck and Left Side: (RS) Rejoin yarn to
center sts. Bind off 51 sts for neck, work to
end—23 sts remain.

(WS) Decrease 1 st at neck edge every row
3 times—20 sts remain. Bind off all sts.

FRONT
Work as for Back through Row 116 of
Chart.

Shape Neck: (RS) Work 31 sts, turn; place
remaining 57 sts on holder for neck and
right side.

Left Side: (WS) Decrease 1 st at neck edge
every row 10 times, then every 4 rows
once—20 sts remain. Work even to end of
Chart. Bind off all sts.

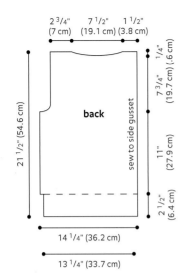

back

2 3/4" (7 cm) 7 1/2" (19.1 cm) 1 1/2" (3.8 cm)

1/4" (.6 cm)

7 3/4" (19.7 cm)

21 1/2" (54.6 cm)

sew to side gusset

11" (27.9 cm)

2 1/2" (6.4 cm)

14 1/4" (36.2 cm)

13 1/4" (33.7 cm)

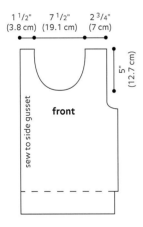

front

1 1/2" (3.8 cm) 7 1/2" (19.1 cm) 2 3/4" (7 cm)

5" (12.7 cm)

sew to side gusset

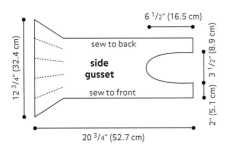

side gusset

sew to back

sew to front

6 1/2" (16.5 cm)

3 1/2" (8.9 cm)

2" (5.1 cm)

12 3/4" (32.4 cm)

20 3/4" (52.7 cm)

Neck and Right Side (RS): Rejoin yarn to sts on holder. Bind off 35 sts for neck, work to end—22 sts remain.

(WS) Decrease 1 st at neck edge every row 10 times, then every 4 rows once—11 sts rem. Bind off all sts.

SIDE GUSSET

Note: Side Gusset is worked sideways and hem is shaped using Short Rows.

Using larger needles and MC, cast on 130 sts; begin Garter st. Work even for 5 rows; place removable marker on RS.

Shape Gusset:

Row 1 (WS): P21, turn.

Rows 2-4: K21, turn, p23, turn, k23, turn.

Rows 5-8, 15-20, 25-28, 33-36, 41-43, 45, 47, 53, 55, 61, 63-65, 71, 73-76, 81-83, 89, 91-93, 99, 101, 107, 109, 111, 113-114, 119-122, 127-130, 135-140, 147-150: Knit across all sts.

Rows 9-14 and 141-146: P15, turn, k15, turn, p16, turn, k16, turn, p17, turn, k17, turn.

Rows 21-24 and 131-134: P18, turn, k18, turn, p19, turn, k19, turn.

Rows 29-32 and 123-126: P21, turn, k21, turn, p23, turn, k23, turn.

Rows 37-40 and 115-118: P12, turn, k12, turn, p14, turn, k14, turn.

Row 44: Bind off 28 sts, knit to end—102 sts remain.

Row 46: Bind off 3 sts, knit to end—99 sts remain.

Row 48, 54, and 56: Bind off 2 sts, knit to end—93 sts remain after Row 56.

Rows 49-52 and 103-106: P16, turn, k16, turn, p18, turn, k18, turn.

Rows 57-60, 67-70, 85-88, and 95-98: P18, turn, k18, turn, p20, turn, k20, turn.

Rows 62, 66, and 72: Bind off 1 st, knit to end—90 sts remain after Row 72.

Rows 77-80: P18, turn, k18, turn, p19, turn, k19, turn.

Rows 84, 90, and 94: Kfb, knit to end—93 sts after Row 94.

Rows 100, 102, and 108: Using Cable Cast-On Method (see page 164), cast on 2 sts, knit to end—99 sts after Row 108.

Row 110: Cast on 3 sts, knit to end—102 sts.

Row 112: Cast on 28 sts, knit to end—130 sts.

Rows 151-154: P21, turn, k21, turn, p23, turn, k23, turn.

Knit 5 rows.

Bind off all sts.

FINISHING

Sew cast-on edge of Gusset to straight side of Front, and bound-off edge of Gusset to straight side of Back. Sew shoulder seams.

Neckband: RS facing, using circ needle and MC, beginning at left shoulder seam, pick up and knit 109 sts along Front neck edge and 59 sts along Back neck edge—168 sts. Join for working in the rnd, being careful not to twist sts; place marker (pm) for beginning of rnd.

Begin 1x1 Rib, as follows: *K1, p1; repeat from * around. Work even for 7 more rnds (8 rnds total).

Bind off all sts in pattern.

Left Armhole Edging: RS facing, using circ needle and MC, pick up and knit 112 sts evenly around armhole edge. Join for working in the rnd; pm for beginning of rnd.

Begin 1x1 Rib as for Neckband. Work even for 6 rnds total.

Bind off all sts in pattern.

Note: No armhole edging is worked for right armhole.

KEY

- ☐ St st – knit on RS, purl on WS.
- ■ MC
- ■ A
- ■ B
- ■ C
- ■ D
- ■ E
- ■ F
- ■ G
- ■ H

Finish a row before putting
your knitting down.

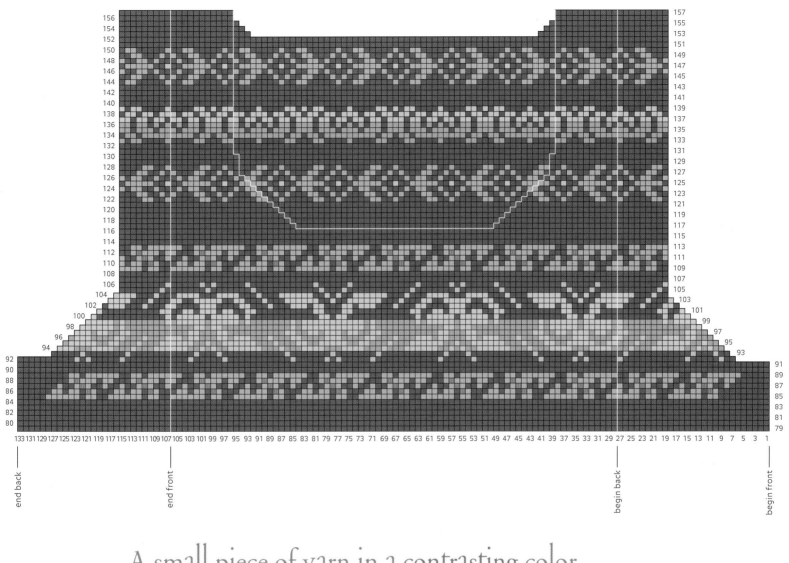

A small piece of yarn in a contrasting color
makes a great stitch marker.

TABLE SKIRT

I made this linen slipcover to place over a garden table that I'd decided to convert into a bedside table. It is knitted in the round with increases to the edge, then drops straight down the sides in a seafoam lace pattern. Ⓜ

SIZE
To fit 16-18" (40.6–45.7 cm) diameter table

FINISHED MEASUREMENTS
80" (203.2 cm) circumference at bound-off edge

YARN
Euroflax Originals Sport Weight (100% linen; 270 yards (247 meters) / 100 grams): 4 hanks #1801 champagne

NEEDLES
One set of 5 double-pointed needles (dpn) size US 4 (3.5 mm)

One 16" (40 cm) circular (circ) needle size US 4 (3.5 mm)

One 24" (60 cm) or 26" (66 cm) circular needle size US 4 (3.5 mm)

Change needle size if necessary to obtain correct gauge.

NOTIONS
Stitch marker

GAUGE
20 sts and 24 rows = 4" (10 cm) in Stockinette stitch (St st)

12 sts and 16 rows = 4" (10 cm) in Seafoam Lace Pattern

NOTES
Skirt will begin in the top center and will be worked in the round to the bottom edges.

Stitch pattern: see page 120.

TABLE SKIRT

Note: When there are too many sts to work comfortably on dpn, transfer sts to 16" circ needle, then to 24" or 26" circ needle as needed.

Using dpn, cast on 8 sts. Divide sts evenly among needles. Join for working in the rnd, being careful not to twist sts; place marker for beginning of rnd.

Rnd 1: *K1-tbl; repeat from * around.

Rnd 2: *Kfb; repeat from * around—16 sts.

Rnd 3 (and all odd-numbered rnds): Knit.

Rnd 4: *K1, kfb; repeat from * around—24 sts.

Rnd 6: *K2, kfb; repeat from * around—32 sts.

Rnd 8: *K3, kfb; repeat from * around—40 sts.

Rnd 10: K2, kfb, *k4, kfb; repeat from * to last 2 sts, k2—48 sts.

Rnd 12: K1, kfb, *k5, kfb; repeat from * to last 4 sts, k4—56 sts.

Rnd 14: K5, kfb, *k6, kfb; repeat from * to last st, k1—64 sts.

Rnd 16: K2, kfb, *k7, kfb; repeat from * to last 5 sts, k5—72 sts.

Rnd 18: K1, kfb, *k8, kfb; repeat from * to last 7 sts, k7—80 sts.

Rnd 20: K6, kfb, *k9, kfb; repeat from * to last 3 sts, k3—88 sts.

Rnd 22: K2, kfb, *k10, kfb; repeat from * to last 8 sts, k8—96 sts.

Rnd 24: K1, kfb, *k11, kfb; repeat from * to last 10 sts, k10—104 sts.

Rnd 26: K7, kfb, *k12, kfb; repeat from * to last 5 sts, k5—112 sts.

Rnd 28: K2, kfb, *k13, kfb; repeat from * to last 11 sts, k11—120 sts.

Rnd 30: K1, kfb, *k14, kfb; repeat from * to last 13 sts, k13—128 sts.

Rnd 32: K8, kfb, *k15, kfb; repeat from * to last 7 sts, k7—136 sts.

Rnd 34: K2, kfb, *k16, kfb; repeat from * to last 14 sts, k14—144 sts.

STITCH PATTERN

SEAFOAM LACE PATTERN

(multiple of 10 sts; 8-rnd repeat)

Rnds 1 and 5: Knit.

Rnds 2 and 6: Purl.

Rnd 3: *[Yo] twice, k1, [yo] 3 times, k1, [yo] 4 times, k1, [yo] 3 times, k1, [yo] twice, k6; repeat from * around.

Rnd 4: Purl, dropping all yo's.

Rnd 7: K5, *[yo] twice, k1, [yo] 3 times, k1, [yo] 4 times, k1, [yo] 3 times, k1, [yo] twice, k6; repeat from * to last 5 sts, [yo] twice, k1, [yo] 3 times, k1, [yo] 4 times, k1, [yo] 3 times, k1, [yo] twice, k1.

Rnd 8: Repeat Rnd 4.

Repeat Rnds 1-8 for Seafoam Lace Pattern.

Rnd 36: K1, kfb, *k17, kfb; repeat from * to last 16 sts, k16—152 sts.

Rnd 38: K9, kfb, *k18, kfb; repeat from * to last 9 sts, k9—160 sts.

Rnd 40: K2, kfb, *k19, kfb; repeat from * to last 17 sts, k17—168 sts.

Rnd 42: K1, kfb, *k20, kfb; repeat from * to last 19 sts, k19—176 sts.

Rnd 44: K10, kfb, *k21, kfb; repeat from * to last 11 sts, k11—184 sts.

Rnd 46: K2, kfb, *k22, kfb; repeat from * to last 20 sts, k20—192 sts.

Rnd 48: K1, kfb, *k23, kfb; repeat from * to last 22 sts, k22—200 sts.

Rnd 50: K11, kfb, *k24, kfb; repeat from * to last 13 sts, k13—208 sts.

Rnd 52: K2, kfb, *k25, kfb; repeat from * to last 23 sts, k23—216 sts.

Rnd 54: K1, kfb, *k26, kfb; repeat from * to last 25 sts, k25—224 sts.

Rnd 56: K12, kfb, *k27, kfb; repeat from * to last 15 sts, k15—232 sts.

Rnd 58: K2, kfb, *k28, kfb; repeat from * to last 26 sts, k26—240 sts.

Purl 1 rnd. Knit 1 rnd. Repeat last 2 rnds twice.

Purl 1 rnd.

Change to Seafoam Lace Pattern. Work Rows 1-8 of pattern 6 times.

Knit 1 rnd. Purl 1 rnd. Repeat last 2 rnds once.

Bind off all sts knitwise. Weave in ends.

Mel Teaches Us to Avoid Hasty Judgments

It's exciting to finish something, and there's always that tense moment when you wonder if it will be everything you'd hoped for. I don't trust myself to know that at first. There have been sweaters I've finished and cried over, only to find that after a few weeks in the cupboard and maybe even a modeling session by my daughter, who has decided she loves it and wants it, it doesn't look so bad after all. My initial negative reaction could have had something to do with my mood at the time I finished it, or the fact that I'd gained a few pounds during the knitting. So if you are disappointed when you first try on a new sweater, set it aside for a short time and revisit it later—don't just throw it onto the dog's bed. You're likely to be happily surprised. Ⓜ

Mel's Theory on Finishing Projects

"Why don't I ever finish anything?" I hear this question from customers all the time. The answer lies in how many unfinished projects you have. Let's face it, yarn is very tempting, like delicious chocolate, pastry, French fries, or anything else that's comforting. You can get carried away. As my mother would say, "Your eyes are too big for your stomach." You see all the tempting colors and softness and are so busy fantasizing about that gorgeous, glamorous new scarf that before you know it, a few more balls of yarn and a pattern have found their way into your stash.

My secret to completing things is not to have too many going at one time. When people ask me how long it will take to finish something, I sometimes say, "As long as you want it to." I've had projects that have taken years, and I've finished a whole sweater in a weekend. Here's the simple fact: If you work at it consistently, a little every day, your project will get finished, but if you have several going at once, each project is going to take longer. I like to have two projects on the needles at one time—an easy one for when I'm with friends and family, watching a movie, or traveling, and another, more demanding one for when I have time to focus. Ⓜ

LADY DETECTIVE HAT

Wearing a hat with a brim makes me feel a little like Miss Marple. This one is jaunty, easy, and fast to make. Finish it with a decorative buckle. I found the plastic one shown here while rummaging through a box of vintage haberdashery supplies at a flea market. There are pretty new ones available, made of mother-of-pearl or rhinestones. Either would work well on this hat. Ⓜ

SIZES
One size

FINISHED MEASUREMENTS
20" (50.8 cm) circumference

YARN
Noro Iro (75% wool / 25% silk; 131 yards (120 meters) / 100 grams): 2 hanks #56 pink/green multi

NEEDLES
One set of five double-pointed needles size US 11 (8 mm)

One 16" (40 cm) circular (circ) needle size US 11 (8 mm)

Change needle size if necessary to obtain correct gauge.

NOTIONS
Stitch marker; 1 decorative buckle with 1-2" opening; 22" grosgrain ribbon (optional)

GAUGE
12 ³/₄ sts and 16 rows = 4" (10 cm) in Purl-Knit Twist Pattern

NOTES
Stitch pattern: see page 124.

When stitching turned hems on the WS, be careful to catch the part of the st that is closest to the WS surface. This will make the hemline less visible on the RS.

HAT

Using dpn, cast on 8 sts. Join for working in the rnd, being careful not to twist sts; place marker for beginning of rnd.

Begin Top of Crown:

Rnd 1: *K1-tbl; repeat from * around.

Rnd 2: *Kfb; repeat from * around—16 sts.

Rnd 3 and all odd-numbered rnds: Purl.

Rnds 4, 8, and 10: Knit.

Rnd 6: *Kfb; repeat from * around—32 sts.

Rnd 12: *Kfb; repeat from * around—64 sts.

Rnd 13: Purl.

Bind off all sts loosely.

Crown: RS facing, using circ needle, pick up and knit 64 sts around bound-off edge; begin Purl-Knit Twist Pattern. Work even until Crown measures 5" from pick-up edge, ending with Rnd 2 or 4 of pattern.

Shape Brim:

Rnd 1: *K3, kfb; repeat from * around—80 sts.

Rnds 2-5: Work Rnds 1-4 of Purl-Knit Twist Pattern.

Rnd 6: Work Rnd 1 of Purl-Knit Twist Pattern.

Rnd 7: *K4, kfb; repeat from * around—96 sts.

Rnds 8-9: Work Rnds 3-4 of Purl-Knit Twist Pattern.

Rnd 10 (fold line): Purl.

Rnds 11 and 12: Knit.

Rnd 13: *K4, k2tog; repeat from * around —80 sts remain.

Rnds 14-18: Knit.

Rnd 19: *K3, k2tog; repeat from * around —64 sts remain.

STITCH PATTERN

PURL-KNIT TWIST PATTERN

(2-st repeat; 4-rnd repeat)

Rnd 1: *P2tog, but do not drop sts from left-hand needle, yb, k2tog the same 2 sts, drop sts from needle together; repeat from * to end of rnd.

Rnd 2: Knit.

Rnd 3: P1, *p2tog, but do not drop sts from left-hand needle, yb, k2tog the same 2 sts, drop sts from needle together; repeat from * to last st, k1.

Rnd 4: Knit.

Repeat Rnds 1-4 for Purl-Knit Twist Pattern.

The Heroin Yarn

A few years ago I made a gray cashmere cardigan. When I bought the yarn, I knew my color had been discontinued but I felt confident that I had enough of it to finish the project. But as I headed up the final arm, I realized with mounting terror that I had misjudged things. The armhole loomed ahead of me, and my final gray ball began to skitter across the floor, getting smaller and smaller. I was running on empty.

Wildfiber was the first to know, of course. "Sorry, Tracey, that color has been discontinued."

I started working the phones. Patti in Pittsburgh was sold out. Betty in Colorado had only ordered the pink, and Amy in Phoenix had never heard of it, "But we have some fun fluffy stuff we've been making dream catchers out of lately."

I Googled it on my computer, typing "GRAY PUTTY CASHMERE" in bold capitals. The search turned up one skein in Ohio. Yes! One would do! One was an armpit and a shoulder seam! But after a consultation with Manny in the stockroom, I was told that an inventory mistake had been made and the yarn wasn't there. Manny was lucky he was in Ohio and I was in Los Angeles.

I began to imagine myself unpicking the cardigan and reknitting it on smaller needles. My brain raced with new gauge calculations. But the sweater was a perfect size for me. It looked great apart from a large hole in the shoulder. Maybe I could stitch a scarf on it in a "casually tossed over" way. I tried to distract myself with other work—a diagonal striped vest, a linen kilt—but I couldn't forget my failure, which I had folded up and hidden in a basket.

A month later I found myself in New York City on a business trip. I was taking a taxi down Madison Avenue one morning and as I waited in traffic, I spied a small glass doorway and inside that stacks of yarn. Before I knew it, I was telling the driver to wait around the corner while I ran into the store. I burst in, startling the young woman behind the counter.

"Do you have one skein of Softly cashmere in putty?" I asked.

Rnds 20 and 21: Knit.

Bind off all sts loosely.

FINISHING

Turn Brim to WS at fold line and sew to base of Crown, being careful not to let sts show on RS.

Strap: Cast on 8 sts; begin St st. Work even for 4". Bind off all sts. Weave in ends. Thread Strap through decorative buckle and sew to side of Crown on RS.

Optional: If Crown is too large, measure circumference of head. Cut length of grosgrain ribbon to fit head plus $1/4$" seam allowance. Sew ribbon to base of Crown on WS. Fold ends of ribbon to back and stitch ends together.

A flicker of recognition crossed the girl's face. "I remember you," she said. "You called about a month ago. You sounded so upset when I told you we were out of that yarn."

As she looked at me sympathetically I noticed a gray speck poking out of a box above her head. A gray, distinctly putty-colored speck! Before I knew it, I was behind the counter and climbing a stepladder, reaching for it. "Ma'am, you can't come behind here!" she protested. But I had, and I was already pulling the speck out of its box and finding that it was connected to a fat skein of putty cashmere!

"The stuff! You did have the stuff, man!" In my relief and delight, I didn't know whether to snort it or knit it.

After apologizing profusely for her mistake, she found another three skeins of the heroin, I mean yarn, and I left triumphantly. The armpit soon bridged the divide with the shoulder seam, and this piece remains my favorite and most-cherished winter wraparound. ⓣ

NOVELLA SOCKS

These cozy cashmere-wool leg warmers, inspired by Elizabethan men's gaiters, have a turned heel that follows the shape of the foot and ends mid-instep. They are knit in the round from the top down in lattice cables with eyelets. Make them with or without the ruffle. **M**

SIZES
Medium (to work larger size, see Note below)

FINISHED MEASUREMENTS
Leg length: 16" (40.6 cm)

Foot circumference: 9 (10)" (22.9 (25.4) cm)

Leg circumference: 8 (9)" (20.3 (22.9) cm)

YARN
Rowan Cashsoft DK (57% wool / 33% microfiber / 10% cashmere; 142 yards (130 meters) / 50 grams): 4 balls #506 crush (Version A, with ruffle) or #502 bella donna (Version B, without ruffle)

NEEDLES
One set of five double-pointed needles (dpn) size US 4 (3.5 mm)

One set of five double-pointed needles size US 5 (3.75 mm)

One set of five double-pointed needles size US 6 (4 mm) (for larger size only)

Change needle size if necessary to obtain correct gauge.

NOTIONS
Crochet hook size F/5 (3.75 mm)

Stitch marker; cable needle (cn); stitch holder

GAUGE
30 sts and 32 rows = 4" (10 cm) in Lattice Pattern using size US 5 needles

26½ sts and 28½ rows = 4" (10 cm) in Lattice Pattern using size US 6 needles (for larger size only)

NOTES
Pattern is written for size Medium. If you wish to make larger size, use larger needle sizes listed.

Stitch patterns and techniques: see page 128.

VERSION A (make 2)

Using smallest needles, cast on 150 sts; divide evenly over 3 needles. Join for working in the rnd, being careful not to twist sts; place marker (pm) for beginning of rnd.

Begin Ruffle:

Rnds 1 and 2: *P3, k7; repeat from * to end.

Rnd 3: *P3, skp, k3, k2tog; repeat from * to end—120 sts remain.

Rnds 4 and 5: *P3, k5; repeat from * to end.

Rnd 6: *P3, skp, k1, k2tog; repeat from * to end—90 sts remain.

Rnds 7 and 8: *P3, k3; repeat from * to end.

Rnd 9: *P3, sk2p; repeat from * to end—60 sts remain.

Rnd 10: *P3, k1; repeat from * to end.

Rnd 11: *P3, mb; repeat from * to end.

Rnds 12 and 13: * P1, k1; repeat from * to end of rnd.

Rnd 14: *P1, k1, yo, k2tog; repeat from * to end.

Rnd 15: Repeat Rnd 12.

Change to size US 5 dpn and Lattice Pattern. Work 5 repeats of pattern.

HEEL

Change to smallest needles, p3, k2. Transfer last 30 sts worked to stitch holder for Instep. Work back and forth on next 30 sts as follows:

Row 1 (RS): Slip 1, k1, *p2, k2, p2, k4; repeat from * to last 8 sts, [p2, k2] twice.

Row 2 and all WS rows: Slip 1, knit the knit sts and purl the purl sts as they face you.

Repeat Rows 1 and 2 until piece measures 2½" from beginning of Heel, ending with a RS row.

Turn Heel:

Row 1 (WS): Slip 1, work as established for 16 sts, p2tog, p1, turn.

Row 2: Slip 1, k5, k2tog, k1, turn.

Row 3: Slip 1, p6, p2tog, p1, turn.

Row 4: Slip 1, k7, k2tog, k1, turn.

STITCH PATTERNS / TECHNIQUES

MB (make bobble)

[K1, p1] twice in next st to increase to 4 sts, turn; p4, turn; k4, turn; p1, p2tog, p1, turn; sk2p—1 st remains.

C3B (right-slanting cable)

Slip next st purlwise to cn, hold to back, k2, p1 from cn.

C3F (left-slanting cable)

Slip next 2 sts purlwise to cn, hold to front, p1, k2 from cn.

C4F (left-slanting cable)

Slip next 2 sts purlwise to cn, hold to front, k2, k2 from cn.

C4B (right-slanting cable)

Slip next 2 sts purlwise to cn, hold to back, k2, k2 from cn.

LATTICE PATTERN

(multiple of 10 sts; 16-rnd repeat)

NOTE: On Rnds 7 and 14, you will work 2 sts from the following rnd. Position beginning of rnd marker as indicated.

Set-Up Rnd: P3, *k4, p6; repeat from * to last 7 sts, k4, p3.

Rnd 1: P2, C3B, C3F, *p4, C3B, C3F; repeat from * to last 2 sts, p2.

Rnds 2, 4, 8, 10, and 12: Knit the knit sts and purl the purl sts as they face you.

Rnd 3: P1, C3B, p2, C3F, *p2, C3B, p2, C3F; repeat from * to last st, p1.

Rnd 5: *C3B, p4, C3F; repeat from * around.

Rnd 6: K2, *p2, [yo] twice, p3tog, p1, k4; repeat from * to last 8 sts, p2, [yo] twice, p3tog, p1, k2.

Rnd 7: K2, p2, p1 into yo from previous row, p1-tbl into yo from previous row, p2, *C4F, p2, (p1, p1-tbl) into yo, p2; repeat from * to last 2 sts, C4F (last 2 sts from Rnd 7 and first 2 sts from Rnd 8). Position marker in middle of cable after it has been worked.

Rnd 9: *C3F, p4, C3B; repeat from * around.

Rnd 11: P1, C3F, *p2, C3B, p2, C3F; repeat from * to last 6 sts, p2, C3B, p1.

Rnd 13: P2, *C3F, C3B, p4; repeat from * to last 8 sts, C3F, C3B, p2.

Rnd 14: P3, *k4, p2, [yo] twice, p3tog, p1; repeat from * to last 7 sts, k4, p2, [yo] twice, p3tog (last st of Rnd 14 and first 2 sts from Rnd 15). Position marker before yo's.

Rnd 15: P1, *C4B, p2, p1 into yo from previous row, p1-tbl into yo from previous row, p2; repeat from * to last 6 sts, C4B, p2, p1 (from Rnd 16). Position marker after last st.

Rnd 16: P1-tbl, knit the knit sts and purl the purl sts as they face you.

Repeat Rnds 1-16 for Lattice Pattern.

INSTEP LATTICE PATTERN

(multiple of 10 sts; 16 rnds)

Note: St count is increased by 1 on Rnd 6 and is restored on Rnd 11.

Rnd 1: *C3F, p4, C3B; repeat from * to end.

Rnds 2, 4, 8, 10, and 12: Knit the knit sts and purl the purl sts as they face you.

Rnd 3: P1, *C3F, p2, C3B, p2; repeat from * to last 9 sts, C3F, p2, C3B, p1.

Rnd 5: P2, *C3F, C3B, p4; repeat from * to last 8 sts, C3F, C3B, p2.

Rnd 6: P2tog, p1, *k4, p2, [yo] twice, p3tog, p1; repeat from * to last 7 sts, k4, p2, [yo] twice, p1.

Rnd 7: P2, *C4F, p2, p1 into yo from previous row, p1-tbl into yo from previous row, p2; repeat from * to last 9 sts, C4F, p2, p1 into yo from previous row, p1-tbl into yo from previous row, p1.

Rnd 9: P1, *C3B, C3F, p4; repeat from * to end.

Rnd 11: *C3B, p2, C3F, p2; repeat from * to last 11 sts, C3B, p2, C3F, p1, p2tog.

Rnd 13: K2, *p4, C3F, C3B; repeat from * to last 8 sts, p4, C3F, p1.

Rnd 14: K2, p2, [yo] twice, p2tog, p1, *k4, p2, [yo] twice, p3tog, p1; repeat from * to last 3 sts, k1, k2tog.

Rnd 15: K2, *p2, p1 into yo from previous row, p1-tbl into yo from previous row, p2, C4B; repeat from * to last 8 sts, p2, p1 into yo from previous row, p1-tbl into yo from previous row, p2, k2.

Rnd 16: Repeat Rnd 2.

Keep a button jar.

Continue as established, working 1 additional st each row before p2tog or k2tog, until 18 sts remain, ending with a RS row.

GUSSET AND FOOT

Using second needle, pick up and knit 10 sts along left side of Heel flap; using third needle, beginning Instep Lattice Pattern, work across 30 Instep sts from holder; using fourth needle, pick up and knit 10 sts along right side of Heel flap, k9 of Heel from first needle. Redistribute sts as follows: Needle 1: 19 sts (remaining 9 sts of Heel and 10 sts picked up from left side of Heel Flap; Needle 2: 30 Instep sts; Needle 3: 19 sts; pm for new beginning of rnd.

Decrease Rnd: On Needle 1, knit to last 3 sts, k2tog, k1; on Needle 2, continue as established in Instep Lattice Pattern; on Needle 3, k1, ssk, knit to end.

Work even for 1 rnd.

Work Decrease Rnd every other rnd as established until 15 sts remain on Needles 1 and 3—60 sts remain.

Work even until Rnd 16 of Instep Lattice Pattern is completed.** Change to 1x1 Rib, as follows: *K1, p1; repeat from * around. Work even for 5 rnds. Bind off all sts in pattern. Weave in ends.

TIES

Make two 30" crochet chains (see page 164). Thread Tie through eyelets at top of Sock. Make 4 Tassels (see page 165) and attach to Ties.

VERSION B (make 2)

Using size US 5 needles, cast on 60 sts; begin Lattice Pattern. Work 6 repeats of pattern. Change to size US 4 needles. Work as for Version A, from beginning of Heel to end of Instep Lace Pattern (**). Bind off all sts.

(see page 164)

Every Instep Tells a Story

I looked at a sock I had knitted recently, and I realized that every segment reminded me of something. I had cast on for the leg while talking to my daughter about neurotic friends and the stubbornness of men. I made a mistake in the heel when I tried to k2tog and watch *Sex in the City* at the same time. I knitted the instep around the wooden table in Mel's shop with three ladies who were in various stages of motherhood. One was trying to get pregnant, and every one at the table was giving her tips for conceiving—like taking her temperature, lighting green candles, and standing on her head (my personal favorite). As I started to decrease for the toe, I talked to the pregnant girl next to me about baby showers, and her fear that her mother-in-law would stay with her after the birth and take over the household. And as I cast off, an infant in a moss-stitch beanie woke up. While his mother breast-fed him, she held the cardigan she was knitting up against him to gauge the size. "Stop growing!" she exclaimed. "Or I'll have to buy another ball."

So many memories in that sock, and a reminder that I need to knit its partner. ⓣ

PEA POD CARDIGAN

This sweet cardigan was inspired by one I made when I was nineteen years old. The pea pod motif is knit only on the front; the back is plain Stockinette stitch. **Ⓜ** TRACEY ADDS: *This cardigan has a lovely period feel. Shoulder pads would give it a Betty Davis look. Small ones mind you, nothing too* Dynasty.

SIZES
To fit 32 (34, 36, 38)" (81.3 (86.4, 91.4, 96.5) cm) bust

Shown in size 32 (81.3 cm)

FINISHED MEASUREMENTS
34 (36, 38, 40)" (86.4 (91.4, 96.5, 101.6) cm) chest

YARN
Rowan Yarn Classic Cashcotton 4 Ply (35% cotton / 25% polyamide / 18% angora / 13% viscose / 9% cashmere; 197 yards (180 meters) / 50 grams): 6 (6, 7, 7) balls #903 seafoam

NEEDLES
One pair straight needles size US 2 (2.75 mm)

One pair straight needles size US 1 (2.5 mm)

One 24" (60 cm) circular (circ) needle size US 1 (2.5 mm)

Change needle size if necessary to obtain correct gauge.

NOTIONS
Stitch markers; cable needle (cn); stitch holder; six ¹/₂" buttons

GAUGE
28 sts and 40 rows = 4" (10 cm) in Stockinette st (St st) using larger needles

32 sts and 40 rows = 4" (10 cm) over Pea Pod Motif using larger needles

NOTES
When working Pea Pod pattern on Fronts, the pattern will shift toward the armhole edge after working a full 30-row repeat. Reposition marker to new beginning of pattern as indicated.

Stitch pattern and techniques: see page 132.

RIGHT FRONT

Using smaller needles, cast on 63 (67, 70, 74) sts; begin 1x1 Rib, as follows: *K1, p1; repeat from * to last 1 (1, 0, 0) st, k1 (1, 0, 0). Next row (WS): Knit the knit sts and purl the purl sts as they face you.

Work even for 4 more rows (6 rows total).

Make Buttonhole: (RS) K1, p1, k1, yo, k2tog, p1, k1, work to end.

Work even until piece measures 3" from the beginning, ending with a WS row.

Establish Pattern: Change to larger needles.

Row 1 (RS): Work in 1x1 Rib over 7 sts, work row 1 of Right-Slanting Pea Pod over next 20 sts, place marker (pm), knit to end.

Row 2: Purl to marker, slip marker (sm), work Right-Slanting Pea Pod over next 20 sts; place remaining 7 sts on holder for Buttonhole Band—56 (60, 63, 67) sts remain.

Work even as established through Row 30 of Right-Slanting Pea Pod.

Next Row (RS): P2, pm, work Right-Slanting Pea Pod over 20 sts, reposition marker, knit to end.

(WS) Purl to first marker, sm, work as established to next marker, knit to end.

Work even as established through Row 30 of Right-Slanting Pea Pod.

Next Row (RS): P4, reposition marker, work Right-Slanting Pea Pod over 20 sts, reposition marker, knit to end.

Work even as established through Row 30 of Right-Slanting Pea Pod.

Next Row (RS): P26, reposition marker, work Right-Slanting Pea Pod over 20 sts, reposition marker, purl to end. *Note: All sts not worked in Pea Pod pattern will now be worked in Rev St st.*

STITCH PATTERNS/TECHNIQUES

MB (make bobble)

[K1, p1, k1] in next st to increase to 3 sts, turn; p3, turn; k3, turn; p1, p2tog, turn; skp—1 st remains.

C2F

Slip next st to cn, hold to front, k1, k1 from cn.

C2F-P

Slip next st to cn, hold to front, p1, k1 from cn.

C2B

Slip next st to cn, hold to back, k1, k1 from cn.

C2B-P

Slip next st to cn, hold to back, k1, p1 from cn.

RIGHT-SLANTING PEA POD

(panel of 20 sts; 30-row repeat)

Row 1 (RS): P18, C2B.
Row 2: P2, k18.
Row 3: P17, C2B-p, k1.
Row 4: P1, k1, p1, k17.
Row 5: P16, [C2B-p] twice.
Row 6: [K1, p1] twice, k16.
Row 7: P15, [C2B-p] twice, p1.

Row 8: K2, p1, k1, p1, k15.
Row 9: P14, C2B-p, p1, k1, p2.
Row 10: [K2, p1] twice, k14.
Row 11: P13, C2B-p, mb, p1, k1, p2.
Row 12: K2, p1, k3, p1, k13.
Row 13: P12, C2B-p, p2, C2B-p, p2.
Row 14: [K3, p1] twice, k12.
Row 15: P11, C2B-p, mb, p1, C2B-p, p3.
Row 16: K4, p1, k3, p1, k11.
Row 17: P10, C2B-p, p2, C2B-p, p4.
Row 18: K5, p1, k3, p1, k10.
Row 19: P9, C2B-p, mb, p1, C2B-p, p5.
Row 20: K6, p1, k3, p1, k9.
Row 21: P8, C2B-p, p2, C2B-p, p6.
Row 22: K7, p1, k3, p1, k8.
Row 23: P7, C2B-p, mb, p1, C2B-p, p7.
Row 24: K8, p1, k3, p1, k7.
Row 25: P7, k1, p2, C2B-p, p8.
Row 26: K9, p1, k2, p1, k7.
Row 27: P7, C2F-p, C2B-p, p9.
Row 28: K10, p2, k8.
Row 29: P8, C2B, p10.
Row 30: Knit.

Repeat Rows 1-30 for Right-Slanting Pea Pod.

LEFT-SLANTING PEA POD

(panel of 20 sts; 30-row repeat)

Row 1 (RS): C2F, p18.
Row 2: K18, p2.

Row 3: K1, C2F-p, p17.
Row 4: K17, p1, k1, p1.
Row 5: [C2F-p] twice, p16.
Row 6: K16, [p1, k1] twice.
Row 7: P1, [C2F-p] twice, p15.
Row 8: K15, [p1, k1] twice, k1.
Row 9: P2, k1, p1, C2F-p, p14.
Row 10: K14, [p1, k2] twice.
Row 11: P2, C2F-p, mb, C2F-p, p13.
Row 12: K13, [p1, k2] twice, k1.
Row 13: P3, k1, p2, C2F-p, p12.
Row 14: K12, [p1, k3] twice.
Row 15: P3, C2F-p, p1, mb, C2F-p, p11.
Row 16: K11, [p1, k3] twice, k1.
Row 17: P4, C2F-p, p2, C2F-p, p10.
Row 18: K10, [p1, k3] twice, k2.
Row 19: P5, C2F-p, p1, mb, C2F-p, p9.
Row 20: K9, [p1, k3] twice, k3.
Row 21: P6, C2F-p, p2, C2F-p, p8.
Row 22: K8, [p1, k3] twice, k4.
Row 23: P7, C2F-p, p1, mb, C2F-p, p7.
Row 24: K7, [p1, k3] twice, k5.
Row 25: P8, C2F-p, p2, k1, p7.
Row 26: K7, p1, k2, p1, k9.
Row 27: P9, C2F-p, C2B-p, p7.
Row 28: K8, p2, k10.
Row 29: P10, C2F, p8.
Row 30: Knit.

Repeat Rows 1-30 for Left-Slanting Pea Pod.

Shape Armhole: (WS) Bind off 4 (6, 6, 6) sts, knit to marker, sm, work to end—52 (54, 57, 61) sts remain.

Next Row (RS): Work as established to second marker, purl to last 2 sts, p2tog—51 (53, 56, 60) sts remain.

(WS) Decrease 1 st at armhole edge every row 5 (7, 10, 12) times—46 (46, 46, 48) sts remain.

Work even for 8 (6, 3, 1) rows (you should have completed Row 16 of Right-Slanting Pea Pod).

Shape Neck: (RS): Continuing in pattern as established, bind off 12 sts this row, then 2 sts every other row 5 times—24 (24, 24, 26) sts remain.

Work even through Row 30 of Right-Slanting Pea Pod.

Next Row (RS): P4, sm, work Right-Slanting Pea Pod over 20 sts, sm, p0 (0, 0, 2).

Work even through Row 10 of Right-Slanting Pea Pod.

Next Row (RS): Increase 1 st at neck edge this row, then every 4 rows 4 times, working increased sts in Rev St st—29 (29, 29, 31) sts.

Work even as established through Row 30 of Right-Slanting Pea Pod.

Next Row (RS): Continuing in Rev St st, work even for 3 rows, increase 1 st at neck edge on first row—30 (30, 30, 32) sts.

Shape Shoulders: (WS) BO 10 sts at armhole edge once, then 10 (10, 10, 11) sts twice.

LEFT FRONT

Work as for right Front, reversing shaping and stitch patterns, and omitting buttonholes. Begin Left-Slanting Pea Pod 36 (40, 43, 47) sts in from right edge on a RS row; begin armhole shaping on a RS row and neck shaping on a WS row.

BACK

Using smaller needles, cast on 119 (127, 133, 141) sts; begin 1x1 Rib, as follows: K1, *p1, k1; repeat from * across. Next row (WS): Knit the knit sts and purl the purl sts as they face you.

Work even until piece measures 3" from the beginning.

Change to larger needles and St st, beginning with a purl row.

Work even until piece measures same as for Front to armhole shaping, ending with a WS row.

Shape Armhole: (RS) Bind off 4 (6, 6, 6) sts at beginning of next 2 rows, then decrease 1 st each side every row 6 (8, 11, 13) times—99 (99, 99, 103) sts remain.

Work even until armhole measures same as for Front to shoulder shaping, ending with a WS row.

Shape Shoulders and Neck: (RS) Right Side: Bind off 10 sts, work 22 (22, 22, 24) sts, turn; place remaining 66 (66, 66, 68) sts on holder for left side.

(WS) Decrease 1 st at neck edge every row 3 times and, AT THE SAME TIME, bind off 10 (10, 10, 11) sts at armhole edge twice.

(RS) Left Side: Rejoin yarn to sts on holder; bind off 33 sts, work to end.

Complete as for right side, reversing shaping.

SHORT SLEEVE (make 2)

Using smaller needles, cast on 82 (84, 88, 88) sts; begin 1x1 Rib, as follows: *K1, p1; repeat from * across. Next row (WS): Knit the knit sts and purl the purl sts as they face you.

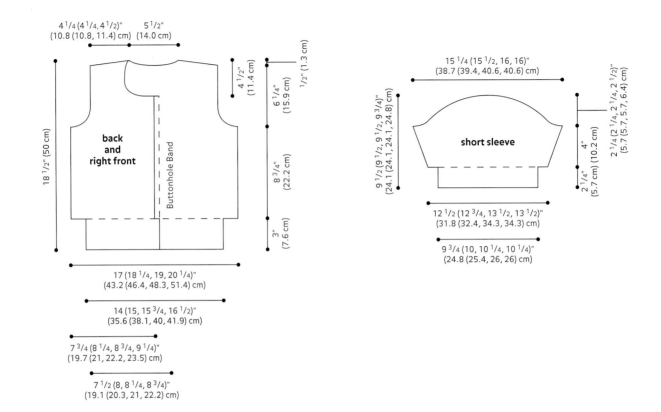

Schematic labels (back and right front):

4 1/4 (4 1/4, 4 1/2)" (10.8 (10.8, 11.4) cm)

5 1/2" (14.0 cm)

4 1/2" (11.4 cm)

1/2" (1.3 cm)

6 1/4" (15.9 cm)

18 1/2" (50 cm)

back and right front

Buttonhole Band

8 3/4" (22.2 cm)

3" (7.6 cm)

17 (18 1/4, 19, 20 1/4)" (43.2 (46.4, 48.3, 51.4) cm)

14 (15, 15 3/4, 16 1/2)" (35.6 (38.1, 40, 41.9) cm)

7 3/4 (8 1/4, 8 3/4, 9 1/4)" (19.7 (21, 22.2, 23.5) cm)

7 1/2 (8, 8 1/4, 8 3/4)" (19.1 (20.3, 21, 22.2) cm)

Schematic labels (short sleeve):

15 1/4 (15 1/2, 16, 16)" (38.7 (39.4, 40.6, 40.6) cm)

9 1/2 (9 1/2, 9 1/2, 9 3/4)" (24.1 (24.1, 24.1, 24.8) cm)

short sleeve

2 1/4 (2 1/4, 2 1/4, 2 1/2)" (5.7 (5.7, 5.7, 6.4) cm)

4" (10.2 cm)

2 1/4" (5.7 cm)

12 1/2 (12 3/4, 13 1/2, 13 1/2)" (31.8 (32.4, 34.3, 34.3) cm)

9 3/4 (10, 10 1/4, 10 1/4)" (24.8 (25.4, 26, 26) cm)

Work even until piece measures 2 1/4" from the beginning.

Next Row (RS): Change to larger needles and St st, beginning with a knit row, increasing 6 sts across first row—88 (90, 94, 94) sts.

Work even for 1 row.

Shape Sleeve: (RS) Continuing in St st, increase 1 st each side this row, then every 4 rows 8 times—106 (108, 112, 112) sts.

Work even until piece measures 6 1/4" from the beginning, ending with a WS row.

Shape Cap: (RS) Bind off 4 (6, 6, 6) sts at beginning of next 2 rows, then decrease 1 st each side every row 8 (8, 8, 10) times, ending with a WS row—82 (80, 84, 80) sts remain.

Next Row (RS): Bind off 6 sts at beginning of next 12 rows—10 (8, 12, 8) sts remain.

Bind off all sts.

FINISHING

Sew shoulders. Sew side and Sleeve seams. Sew in Sleeves.

Buttonhole Band: (WS) Rejoin yarn to sts on holder for right Front; work in 1x1 Rib as established for 3 rows, ending with a WS row.

(RS) Make Buttonhole this row, then every 26 rows 3 times, as follows: K1, p1, k1, yo, k2tog, p1, k1. Work even for 23 rows; place sts on holder for Neckband. Sew Band to Front edge.

Button Band: Rejoin yarn to sts on holder for left Front; work even as for Buttonhole Band, omitting buttonholes, until piece measures same as for Buttonhole Band; place sts on holder for Neckband. Sew Band to Front edge.

Neckband: RS facing, using circ needle, and beginning at Buttonhole Band, work in 1x1 Rib across 7 sts from holder, pick up and knit 49 sts along right Front neck edge, 39 sts along Back neck edge, 49 sts along left Front neck edge, then work in 1x1 Rib across 7 sts from holder—151 sts.

(WS) Work even in 1x1 Rib for 2 rows.

Make Buttonhole: (WS) Work to last 7 sts, p1, k1, p1, yo, p2tog, k1, p1.

Work even for 2 rows. Bind off all sts in pattern.

Sew buttons opposite buttonholes. Weave in ends.

Unraveling

Here's the thing with knitting—it won't always go the way you want it to. For instance, you get forty rows into a piece and realize you are following a pattern incorrectly and are gaining three stitches every other row. It still looks kind of okay, but you are definitely flying blind. You look at it and say, "Hmm, well, if I stretched some sections out a bit when they're finished and sewed the seams a little tighter, it would probably look fine." But would it? Who are you fooling! It's painful, but at a moment like this, you just have to take a deep breath, pull the yarn off the needles, and start winding it back the other way.

If you still need persuading, imagine that the piece is like a relationship, and ask yourself these questions. Would I continue to date a confusing, deceptive, strangely-slanted man who makes me feel sloppy, incompetent, and fat? A guy that's no fun to show off to my friends, because they keep pointing out his flaws, and when I ask him to change, he says, "I can't, I'm just not made that way"?

Of course you wouldn't. You'd dump a guy like that! You might feel bad at first, but you'd learn from your mistakes and start a new relationship with someone worthy of you. Unless you're over fifty and live in Los Angeles, in which case you'd hang onto him for dear life—and knit an age-inappropriate thong bikini. **T**

Jacket: to fit 34 (36, 38, 40-42)" (86.4 (91.4, 96.5, 101.6-104.7) cm) bust

Skirt: to fit 26-28 (30, 32, 34)" (66-71.1 (76.2, 81.3, 86.4) cm) waist; 35 (36, 38, 39)" (88.9 (91.4, 96.5, 99.1) cm) hip

Shown in size 34" (86.4 cm) jacket and 26-28" (66-71.1 cm) skirt

FINISHED MEASUREMENTS
Jacket: 33 1/2 (36 1/2, 39 1/2, 42)" (85.1 (92.7, 100.3, 106.7) cm) chest

Skirt: 29 3/4 (31 1/4, 32 3/4, 34)" (75.6 (79.4, 83.2, 87) cm) low waist; 19 (20, 20, 20)" (48.3 (50.8, 53.3, 55.9) cm) long

YARN
Karabella Yarns Aurora 8 (100% extra fine merino wool; 98 yards (90 meters) / 50 grams): 18 (18, 18, 19) balls #276 celery or #754 aquamarine for jacket; 10 (11, 11, 11) balls #276 celery for skirt

NEEDLES
Jacket: One pair straight needles size US 7 (4.5 mm)

One pair straight needles size US 8 (5 mm)

One 24" (60 cm) circular (circ) needle size US 7 (4.5 mm)

Skirt: One each 29" (74 cm) and 36" (91 cm) circular needle size US 7 (4.5 mm)

One each 29" (74 cm) and 36" (91 cm) circular needle size US 8 (5 mm)

NOTIONS
Stitch holders (4); stitch markers; six 1" buttons (jacket); 1 yard 1" elastic

GAUGE
22 sts and 28 rows = 4" (10 cm) in Scallop st using larger needles

NOTES
Slip all sts purlwise wyib.

When stitching turned hems on the WS, catch the part of the st that is closest to the WS surface to make hemline less visible on RS.

Stitch patterns: see page 138.

PONSONBY SUIT

This project began as an all-purpose cozy but elegant jacket. But once I finished knitting the jacket, I couldn't resist making a skirt to match. The jacket is knit in a diagonal scallop pattern and has self-lined lapels, which are worked as you go. The skirt is knit in the round and has a comfortable elastic waist. I named the suit after Ponsonby, a chic neighborhood in Auckland, New Zealand, where there are always stylish and well-dressed women sitting in the cafes. Ⓜ TRACEY TELLS US: *The dogs in this photograph are my spaniels, Frankie and Stella. Frankie, the redhead, disgraced herself recently by ripping a ball of white angora to shreds. She must have thought it was a rabbit or something. Well, the lady from Alabama who sold her to me did say, "She's beautiful but she hasn't got a lot going on upstairs, honey."*

JACKET
BACK
LEFT PANEL
Note: When casting on sts at the beginning of a row for hem facings and plackets, use the Knitted Cast-On method (see page 164).

Using smaller needles, cast on 22 (26, 30, 34) sts. Work even in St st for 5 rows, beginning with a purl row.

(RS) Purl 1 row (fold line). Purl 1 row.

Next Row (RS): Slip 1, knit to end.

Establish Pattern:

Row 1 (WS): P1, work Row 1 of Scallop st across center 20 (24, 28, 32) sts, p1.

Row 2: Slip 1, work in Scallop st to last st, k1.

Row 3: P1, work in Scallop st to last st, p1.

Row 4: Change to larger needles, cast on 4 sts for hem facing, knit these 4 cast-on sts, slip 1, work in Scallop st to last st, k1—26 (30, 34, 38) sts.

Row 5: P1, work in Scallop st to last 5 sts, p5.

Row 6: K4, slip 1, work in Scallop st to last st, k1.

Work even until piece measures approximately 5" from fold line, ending with Row 3 of Scallop st.

Next Row (RS): Bind off 5 sts, work in

STITCH PATTERNS

BIND 2

With the tip of the right-hand needle inserted from back to front, lift the strand between the two needles onto the right-hand needle; knit the next 2 sts, pass the lifted strand over the 2 knit sts and off the needle.

SCALLOP ST

(multiple of 4 sts; 4-row repeat)
Rows 1 and 3 (WS): Purl.
Row 2: *Bind 2, k2; repeat from * to end.
Row 4: *K2, bind 2; repeat from * to end.
Repeat Rows 1-4 for Scallop st.

SCALLOP ST IN-THE-ROUND

(multiple of 4 sts; 4-rnd repeat)
Rnds 1 and 3: Knit.
Rnd 2: *Bind 2, k2; repeat from * around.
Rnd 4: *K2, bind 2; repeat from * around.
Repeat Rnds 1-4 for Scallop st in-the-round.

Scallop st to last st, k1—21 (25, 29, 33) sts remain.

Work even for 1 row. Place sts on holder for Back.

CENTER PANEL

Using smaller needles, cast on 50 sts. Work first 7 rows as for Left Panel.

(RS) Slip 1, knit to end, slip 1.

Establish Pattern:

Row 1 (WS): P1, work Row 1 of Scallop st across center 48 sts, p1.

Row 2: Slip 1, work in Scallop st to last st, slip 1.

Row 3: Cast on 4 sts for hem facing, purl these 4 cast-on sts, p1, work in Scallop st to last st, p1—54 sts.

Row 4: Change to larger needles; cast on 4 sts for hem facing, knit these 4 cast-on sts, slip 1, work in Scallop st to last 5 sts, slip 1, k4—58 sts.

Row 5: P5, work in Scallop st to last 5 sts, p5.

Work even until piece measures approximately 5" from fold line, ending with Row 3 of pattern.

Next Row (RS): Bind off 4 sts at beginning of next 2 rows—50 sts remain. Place sts on holder.

RIGHT PANEL

Work as for Left Panel until 7 rows are completed.

Next Row (RS): Knit to last st, slip 1.

Establish Pattern:

Row 1 (WS): P1, work Row 1 of Scallop st across center 20 (24, 28, 32) sts, p1.

Row 2: K1, work in Scallop st to last st, slip 1.

Row 3: Cast on 4 sts for hem facing, purl these 4 cast-on sts, p1, work in Scallop st to last st, p1—26 (30, 34, 38) sts.

Row 4: Change to larger needles, work in Scallop st to last 5 sts, slip 1, k4.

Row 5: P5, work in Scallop st to last st, p1.

Row 6: K1, work in Scallop st to last 5 sts, slip 1, k4.

Work even until piece measures approximately 5" from fold line, ending with Row 4 of Scallop st.

Next Row (WS): Bind off 5 sts, work in Scallop st to last st, k1—21 (25, 29, 33) sts remain.

Do not break yarn.

JOIN PANELS

RS facing, using larger needles, transfer Panels to left-hand needle as follows: 21 (25, 29, 33) sts of Left Panel, 50 sts of Center Panel, and 21 (25, 29, 33) sts of Right Panel—92 (100, 108, 116) sts.

Establish Pattern:

Row 1 (RS): Using yarn attached to Right Panel, k1, work in Scallop st as established across 20 (24, 28, 32) sts, slip 1, work in Scallop st as established across 48 sts, slip 1, work in Scallop st as established across 20 (24, 28, 32) sts, k1. Continue even, working Scallop st panels as established, and purling slipped sts on WS rows, until piece measures 6" from fold line, ending with a WS row.

Shape Waist: (RS) Decrease 1 st each side this row, then every 12 rows once—88

(96, 104, 112) sts remain. Work even for 11 rows.

(RS) Increase 1 st each side this row, then on following 12th row, working increased sts in pattern as they become available—92 (100, 108, 116) sts.

Work even until piece measures 16 (17, 18, 18 1/2)" or desired length from fold line, ending with a WS row.

Shape Armholes: (RS) Bind off 4 (5, 6, 6) sts at beginning of next 2 rows, then decrease 1 st each side every row 6 (8, 8, 12) times—72 (74, 80, 80) sts remain.

Work even until armhole measures 8 (8, 9, 9)", ending with a WS row.

Next Row (RS): Bind off 11 (11, 12, 12) sts, work 11 (11, 12, 12) sts, turn.

Bind off 1 st, work to end.

Bind off remaining 11 (11, 12, 12) sts.

RS facing, rejoin yarn to remaining sts. Bind off 26 (28, 30, 30) sts, work to end—23 (23, 25, 25) sts remain.

(WS) Bind off 11 (11, 12, 12) sts purlwise, work to end—12 (12, 13, 13) sts remain.

Bind off 1 st, work to end. Bind off remaining 11 (11, 12, 12) sts purlwise.

POCKET LININGS (make 2)
Using smaller needles, cast on 22 sts. Work even in St st for 4 1/2", ending with a WS row. Place sts on holder for Front.

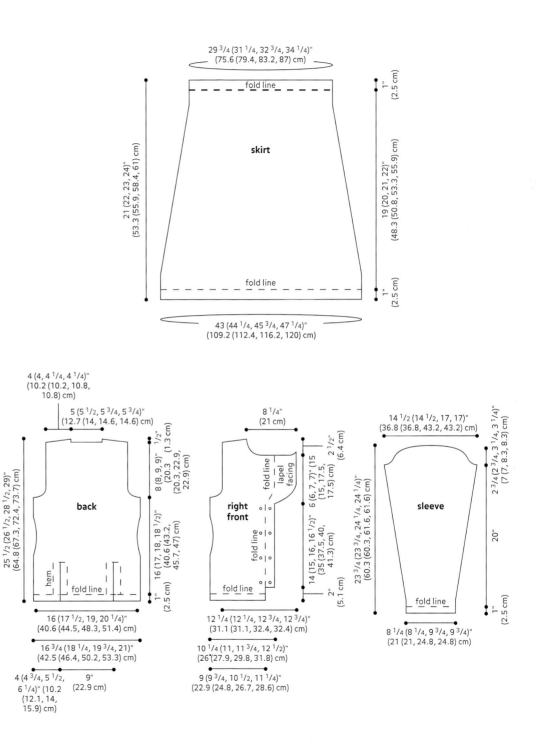

(WS) Work even until piece measures approximately 6" from fold line, ending with Row 2 of Scallop st.

Shape Waist: (WS) Decrease 1 st, work to end—56 (60, 64, 68) sts remain.

Insert Pocket Lining: (RS) Work 24 (26, 28, 30) sts, slip next 22 sts to holder for Pocket, leave at front of work; continuing in Scallop st as established, work across 22 sts of Pocket Lining, work to end.

Work even for 10 rows.

(WS) Decrease 1 st, work to end—55 (59, 63, 67) sts remain. Work even for 11 rows.

(WS) Increase 1 st at beginning of row this row, then on following 12th row, working increased sts in pattern as they become available—57 (61, 65, 69) sts.

Work even until piece measures 14 (15, 16, 16 1/2)" or desired length from fold line, ending with a WS row.

Shape Neck: (RS) Kfb, work in Scallop st across 6 sts *(Note: Second repeat will not be complete)*, m1, slip 1, m1, work to end—60 (64, 68, 72) sts. Work even for 1 row.

(RS) Increase 3 sts as established this row, every other row once, then every 4 rows 4 times, working increased sts in Scallop st as they become available and, AT THE SAME TIME, when piece measures same as for Back to armhole,

Shape Armhole: (WS) Bind off 4 (5, 6, 6) sts, work to end. Decrease 1 st at armhole edge every row 6 (8, 8, 12) times.

RIGHT FRONT

Using smaller needles, cast on 50 (54, 58, 62) sts. Work first 7 rows as for Left Panel.

(RS) Slip 1, knit to end.

Establish Pattern:

Row 1 (WS): P1, work Row 1 of Scallop st across center 48 (52, 56, 60) sts, p1.

Row 2: Slip 1, work in Scallop st to last st, k1.

Row 3: P1, work in Scallop st to last st, p1.

Row 4: Change to larger needles; cast on 7 sts for Buttonhole Placket, knit these 7 cast-on sts, slip 1, work in Scallop st to last st, k1—57 (61, 65, 69) sts.

Row 5: P1, work to last 8 sts, p8.

Row 6: K7, slip 1, work to last st, k1.

Row 7: Repeat Row 5.

Buttonhole Row (RS): K3, yo, k2tog, k2, slip 1, work 4 sts in Scallop st as established, yo, k2tog, work as established to end. Repeat Buttonhole every 28 rows 3 times, and AT THE SAME TIME,

Continuing neck edge increases as established, work even until armhole measures 6 (6, 7, 7)", ending with a RS row—68 (69, 72, 72) sts remain.

Next Row (WS): Work 37 (38, 41, 41) sts, turn. Place remaining 31 sts on holder for Placket.

(RS) BO 5 sts, work to end—32 (33, 36, 36) sts remain.

(WS) Decrease 1 st at neck edge every row 10 (11, 12, 12) times—22 (22, 24, 24) sts remain.

Work even until armhole measures 8 (8, 9, 9)", ending with a RS row.

Next Row (WS): Bind off 11 (11, 12, 12) sts, work to end—11 (11, 12, 12) sts remain. Work even for 1 row.

Bind off all sts.

Shape Placket: (WS) Rejoin yarn to sts on holder, bind off 25 sts, work to end—6 sts remain.

(RS) Decrease 1 st at neck edge every row 5 times—1 st remains. Fasten off.

LEFT FRONT

Work as for Right Front until 7 rows are completed.

(RS) Knit to last st, slip 1.

Establish Pattern:

Row 1 (WS): P1, work Row 1 of Scallop st across center 48 (52, 56, 60) sts, p1.

Row 2: K1, work in Scallop st to last st, slip 1.

Row 3: Cast on 7 sts for Button Placket, purl these 7 cast-on sts, p1, work in Scallop st to last st, p1—57 (61, 65, 69) sts.

Row 4: Change to larger needles; k1, work in Scallop st to last 8 sts, slip 1, k7.

Row 5: P8, work to last st, p1.

Row 6: K1, work to last 8 sts, slip 1, k7.

Row 7: Repeat Row 5.

(RS) Work even until piece measures approximately 6" from fold line, ending with Row 3 of pattern.

Shape Waist and Insert Pocket Lining: (RS) Decrease 1 st, work 9 (11, 13, 15) sts, slip next 22 sts to holder for Pocket, leave at front of work; continuing in Scallop st as established, work across 22 sts of Pocket Lining, work to end—56 (60, 64, 68) sts remain.

Work even for 11 rows.

(RS) Decrease 1 st, work to end—55 (59, 63, 67) sts remain. Work even for 11 rows.

(RS) Increase 1 st at beginning of row this row, then on following 12th row, working increased sts in pattern as they become available—57 (61, 65, 69) sts.

Work even until piece measures 14 (15, 16, 16 1/2)" or desired length from fold line, ending with a WS row.

Shape Neck: (RS) Work in Scallop st to last 8 sts, m1, slip 1, m1, work in Scallop st to last st *(NOTE: second repeat will not be complete)*, kfb—60 (64, 68, 72) sts. Work even for 1 row.

(RS) Increase 3 sts as established this row, every other row once, then every 4 rows 4 times, working increased sts in Scallop st as they become available and, AT THE SAME TIME, when piece measures same as for Back to armhole,

Shape Armhole: (RS) Bind off 4 (5, 6, 6) sts, work to end. Decrease 1 st at armhole edge every row 6 (8, 8, 12) times.

Continuing neck edge increases as established, work even until armhole measures 6 (6, 7, 7)", ending with a WS row—68 (69, 72, 72) sts remain.

Next Row (RS): Work 37 (38, 41, 41) sts, turn. Place remaining 31 sts on holder for Placket.

(WS) BO 5 sts, work to end—32 (33, 36, 36) sts remain.

(RS) Decrease 1 st at neck edge every row 10 (11, 12, 12) times—22 (22, 24, 24) sts remain.

Work even until armhole measures 8 (8, 9, 9)", ending with a WS row.

Next Row (RS): Bind off 11 (11, 12, 12) sts, work to end—11 (11, 12, 12) sts remain. Work even for 1 row.

Bind off all sts.

Shape Placket: (RS) Rejoin yarn to sts on holder, bind off 25 sts, work to end—6 sts remain.

(WS) Decrease 1 st at neck edge every row 5 times—1 st remains. Fasten off.

SLEEVES (make 2)

Using smaller needles, cast on 46 (46, 54, 54) sts. Work first 7 rows as for Left Panel.

(RS) Knit 1 row.

Establish Pattern:

Row 1 (WS): P1, work Row 1 of Scallop st across center 44 (44, 52, 52) sts, p1.

Row 2: K1, work in Scallop st to last st, k1.

Work even for 1 row.

(RS) Change to larger needles; work even for 6 rows.

Shape Sleeve: (RS) Increase 1 st each side this row, then every 6 rows 16 (16, 19, 19) times, working increased sts in Scallop st pattern as they become available—80 (80, 94, 94) sts.

Work even until piece measures 20" or desired length from fold line, ending with a WS row.

Shape Cap: (RS) Bind off 4 (4, 6, 6) sts at beginning of next 2 rows, then 3 sts at beginning of next 8 (8, 10, 10) rows—48 (48, 52, 52) sts remain.

(RS) Decrease 1 st each side every row 10 times—28 (28, 32, 32) sts remain.

Bind off all sts loosely.

FINISHING

Sew shoulder seams.

COLLAR

Fold Front Placket and lapel along slip st edge so that RS's are together. Sew across bound off sts. Turn RS out, matching top edge to line of neck shaping.

WS of Front facing (RS of lapel), using smaller needles, beginning at end of lapel seam of left Front, pick up and knit 11 sts along lapel, 10 sts to shoulder seam, 1 st at shoulder seam, 26 (28, 30, 30) sts along back neck, 1 st at shoulder seam, 10 sts to lapel, and 11 sts to end of lapel seam—70 (72, 74, 74) sts. Purl 1 row.

Next Row (RS): Work in Scallop st across 21 sts, pm, slip 1, pm, work in Scallop st across 26 (28, 30, 30) sts, pm, slip 1, pm, work in Scallop st to end. Work even for 3 rows, slipping sts between markers on RS row.

Increase Row (RS): *Work in Scallop st to marker, m1, slip marker (sm), slip 1, sm, m1; repeat from * once, work to end—74 (76, 78, 78) sts. Work even for 1 row.

(RS) Repeat Increase Row once—78 (80, 82, 82) sts.

Work even for 12 rows.

(WS) Knit 1 row (fold line). Knit 1 row.

Work even in Scallop st for 7 rows.

Decrease Row (RS): *Work to 2 sts before marker, k2tog, sm, slip 1, sm, ssk; repeat from * once, work to end—74 (76, 78, 78) sts remain. Work even for 1 row.

(RS) Repeat Decrease Row once—70 (72, 74, 74) sts remain.

Work even for 7 rows. Bind off all sts.

Turn Collar at fold line and sew to RS of neckline.

POCKET EDGING

RS facing, slip Pocket sts from holder onto smaller needles.

Work even in Scallop st as established for 5 rows.

(WS) Knit 1 row (fold line). Knit 1 row.

Work even in Scallop st for 7 rows. Bind off all sts loosely.

Press Pocket Lining lightly; sew to WS of Front, being careful not to let sts show on RS.

Turn Pocket Edging to WS at fold line. Sew in place.

Sew sleeve and side seams.

Turn all hems to WS and sew in place, being careful to sew cast-on edges of hem and Plackets to each other so that they do not overlap. Sew in sleeves. Sew buttons opposite buttonholes, and just above Back Panel joins.

PATCH POCKET (optional)

Using larger needles, cast on 18 sts; begin

Scallop st, as follows: P1 (edge st, keep in St st), work in Scallop st to last st, p1 (edge st, keep in St st).

Work even for 3 1/2", ending with Row 2 or 4 of pattern.

Change to smaller needles. Knit 1 row (fold line). Knit 1 row.

Work even in Scallop st for 8 rows. Knit 1 row. Purl 1 row.

Bind off all sts.

Fold top edge of Pocket to WS at fold line and sew in place, being careful not to let sts show on RS.

Sew to left Front, with top edge 3" above beginning of underarm.

SKIRT

Note: Change to 29" circ needle when necessary for number of sts remaining.

Using smaller 36" circ needle, cast on 236 (244, 252, 260) sts. Join for working in the rnd, being careful not to twist sts; pm for beginning of rnd. Begin St st. Work even for 6 rnds.

Purl 1 rnd (fold line).

Establish Pattern:

Setup Rnd: *K58 (60, 62, 64), pm, k1, pm; repeat from * around.

Rnd 1: *Work in Scallop st in-the-rnd to next marker, sm, slip 1, sm; repeat from * around.

Rnd 2: *Work in Scallop st in-the-rnd to next marker, sm, k1, sm; repeat from * around.

Repeat Rnds 1 and 2 once.

Change to larger 36" circ needle and work even for 8 rnds, slipping the st between the markers on Rnds 1 and 3 of pattern and knitting the st on Rnds 2 and 4.

Decrease Rnd: Continuing in pattern as established, *k2tog, knit to 2 sts before marker, ssk, sm, slip 1, sm; repeat from * around—228 (236, 244, 252) sts remain.

Repeat Decrease Rnd every 8 rnds twice, every 22 rnds 3 times, then every 10 rnds 3 times—164 (172, 180, 188) sts remain.

Work even until piece measures 19 (20, 20, 20)" or desired length from fold line.

Change to smaller 29" needle. Knit 1 rnd. Purl 1 rnd (fold line).

Knit 7 rnds. Bind off all sts.

Turn hem at fold line and sew to WS, being careful not to let sts show on RS.

Measure your waist. Cut length of elastic 1-2" shorter than waist measurement and sew ends together. Fold Waistband over elastic to WS and sew in place, being careful not to let sts show on RS.

KNIT 2 TOGETHER SWEATER

Tracey and I love to knit, and we certainly like to knit together, so the inevitable happened. . . . **M** TRACEY PREDICTS: *I can see couples all over America knitting "The Knit 2 Together." It's going to lower divorce rates.*

SIZES
To fit 2 medium-sized people

FINISHED MEASUREMENTS
74" (188 cm) chest

YARN
GGH Goa (50% cotton / 50% HB acrylic; 65 yards (60 meters) / 150 grams): 22 balls #25 blue

NEEDLES
One 47" (120 cm) circular (circ) needle size US 10 (6 mm)

One 26" (66 cm) or 29" (74 cm) circular needle size US 10 (6 mm)

One pair straight needles size US 10 (6mm), for sleeves

One 16" (40 cm) circular needle size US 9 (5.5 mm)

Change needle size if necessary to obtain correct gauge.

NOTIONS
Stitch marker; stitch holders

GAUGE
12 sts and 19 rows = 4" (10 cm) in Stockinette st (St st) using larger needle

BODY

Using longest circ needle, cast on 224 sts. Join for working in the rnd, being careful not to twist sts; place marker (pm) for beginning of rnd. Begin St st.

Work even until piece measures 18" from the beginning.

Divide for Front and Back:

Shape Armholes: Bind off 3 sts, k108, turn; place remaining 112 sts on 29" circular needle for Back—109 sts remain.

FRONT

Working back and forth, bind off 3 sts, purl to end—106 sts remain.

Work even until armhole measures 8", ending with a WS row. Transfer sts to shorter circular needle.

BACK

Rejoin yarn to sts on circular needle for Back. Work as for Front. Leave sts on needle and set aside.

SLEEVES (make 2)

Using larger straight needles, cast on 28 sts. Work in St st for 5 rows, beginning with a purl row.

Shape Sleeve: (RS) Increase 1 st each side this row, every 6 rows 4 times, then every 8 rows 6 times—50 sts.

Work even until piece measures 19" from the beginning.

Bind off all sts.

FINISHING

Lay piece flat with RS of Front facing. Beginning at left Front shoulder, using Kitchener st (see page 164), graft the first 14 sts of Front and Back together for left shoulder. Place next 24 sts of Front and Back on separate holders for left neck opening. Using Kitchener st, graft next (center) 30 sts of Front and Back together for center shoulders. Place next 24 sts of Front and Back on separate holders for right neck opening. Using Kitchener st, graft the last 14 sts of Front and Back together for right shoulder.

Neckbands: Using smaller circ needle, beginning at shoulder seam, pick up and knit 1 st from shoulder seam, knit across 24 sts from Front neck holder, pick up and knit 1 st from shoulder seam, knit across 24 sts from Back neck holder—50 sts. Join for working in the rnd; pm for beginning of rnd. Begin St st. Work even for 2". Bind off all sts. Repeat for second neckband.

Sew sleeve seams. Sew in sleeves.

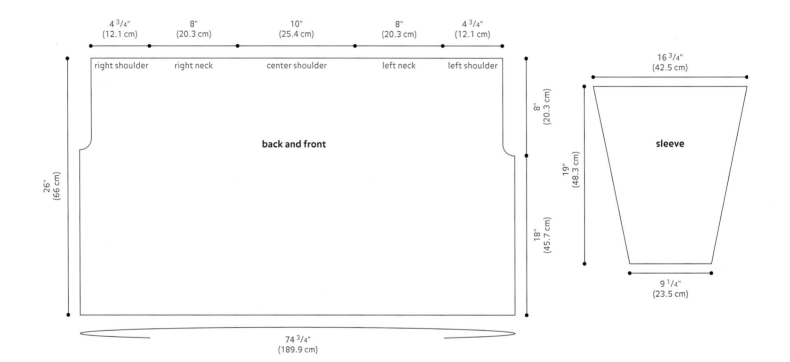

right shoulder | right neck | center shoulder | left neck | left shoulder

4 3/4" (12.1 cm) 8" (20.3 cm) 10" (25.4 cm) 8" (20.3 cm) 4 3/4" (12.1 cm)

back and front

26" (66 cm)

74 3/4" (189.9 cm)

sleeve

16 3/4" (42.5 cm)

8" (20.3 cm)

19" (48.3 cm)

18" (45.7 cm)

9 1/4" (23.5 cm)

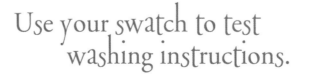

Use your swatch to test washing instructions.

KNITTING BASICS

Getting Started . . .

TRACEY: What's the best sort of yarn to learn to knit with, Mel?

MEL: A plain, untextured yarn is best, in a medium weight, not too chunky and not too thin. I recommend something suitable for a size 8 to 10 needle. There are hundreds of tempting fluffy, sparkly yarns available these days, but starting with one of these will be like trying to put on your lipstick without a mirror.

TRACEY: What about that jumbo, dollar-a-mile synthetic stuff to practice on?

MEL: Some people think that's a good idea, but cheap yarn can be a false economy. Knitting is a very tactile thing. Work with something you like touching, in a color you love to look at, and you'll get a lot more enjoyment out of the process and the final product.

TRACEY: Balls, hanks, skeins, take your pick. But it is hard to wind a hank into a ball on your own, isn't it?

MEL: Wind the yarn around your knees.

TRACEY: Of course! Before I learned the knee technique, I stuck my legs in the air and held the yarn around my ankles as I wound it. It was exhausting but good for the abs.

A Message from Mel

You can get as much as you want out of knitting. I think of it as a part of my journey through life. Every day I learn more, and I always learn from my mistakes. Trying new things in knitting has helped me take risks in other parts of my life. It's empowering to try something new and know that you can succeed at it. From my first wobbly scarf, knitting has kept me passionately interested and excited. How else could I work in a knitting store all day and be excited to rush home and knit!

I confess that I'm an addict, but it's a healthy addiction, and one that gives me and everyone else in my life a lot of pleasure because there is always something new to knit.

If you're thinking that you just want to make simple scarves and not bother to learn more about the intricacies of knitting, that's fine, but you won't know what fun you're missing unless you delve into the mysteries of the stitch. Ⓜ

TRACEY: What needles do you prefer, Mel?

MEL: My favorites are bamboo, wood, or plastic.

TRACEY: I like the circular ones as you can leave your stitches safely on the connecting nylon wire, and you don't move your elbows up and down like a jockey when you knit with them.

MEL: They are also great for casting on hundreds of stitches that wouldn't fit comfortably on straight needles. But to begin with, I recommend straights. They're less confusing. Needles come in different lengths and diameters. Generally, a chunky yarn will need a larger diameter needle and a fine yarn will need a smaller one. A suggested needle size is printed on most yarn labels.

TRACEY: Mel, I always hate it when I read "check the gauge" in a pattern. Because I just want to get on and knit—not do a math equation, which was never my strong suit.

MEL: I can't stress enough how important it is to knit a sample swatch and check your gauge. You can get into so much trouble if you don't. It's really easy. Probably third-grade math. You got through third grade, didn't you, Tracey? You make a square of knitting—about 4 inches—in your desired stitch. After you bind off, you measure the width. Then divide the number of stitches by the width, and there you have it, the gauge, or stitches per inch.

Here's an example. Let's say you want to make a scarf.
● Cast on 20 stitches and make a square in your desired stitch. Bind off.
● Measure the width of your swatch. Let's say it is 4" wide.
● Divide the number of stitches: 20
● By the width of swatch: 4"
● And you have your gauge: 5 stitches per inch.
● If you want to make a 6" wide scarf, you multiply 6 (desired width) x gauge (5 stitches per inch) = 30 stitches.
● To make the scarf, you cast on 30 stitches and work to the desired length.

TRACEY: So, we've got some delicious wool and a pair of shiny smooth needles. Let's cast on.

US and European Needle Sizes

Reading a yarn label can sometimes be confusing because of the different terminology used in the United States and abroad. For example, sometimes the label for a yarn made in Europe will only include the metric needle size. When this is the case, you need to find out the US equivalent. Sometimes the conversion is given on the needle itself and/or on the packaging. If not, you can refer to the chart below or you can use a needle gauge marked with both sizing systems.

A Note from Tracey
When I started knitting, the different sizing system for needles in Europe and the United States constantly confused me. I felt like an American in Paris saying, "Excusez-moi, Monsieurrrrr, but how many inches in a kilometerrrrr?"

NEEDLE SIZE CHART

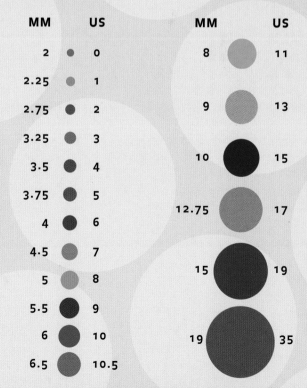

MM	US		MM	US
2	0		8	11
2.25	1		9	13
2.75	2		10	15
3.25	3		12.75	17
3.5	4		15	19
3.75	5		19	35
4	6			
4.5	7			
5	8			
5.5	9			
6	10			
6.5	10.5			

Casting On

To start knitting, you need to put the first row of stitches onto the needle. This is called casting on.

1. Make a slipknot 40" from the end of the ball. To do this, make a circle, then pull the yarn through the circle into a loop that can be tightened or loosened. This is a slipknot. Slide the slipknot onto one of the knitting needles.

2. Holding the needle in your right hand, take your left hand and place your index finger and thumb through the "window" between the two strands of yarn.

3. Drop the needle down between your thumb and index finger so that it forms an "M." Close this off with your remaining fingers into a "heart" shape. Your fingers will hold the yarn steady to create some tension when you cast on a stitch.

   Slide your needle into the front of the loop on your thumb, then into the back of the loop on your index finger. (See arrows on photo below.)

4. Slide the thumb loop over the needle.

5. Pull tight to reveal the cast-on stitch.

6. Repeat steps 2–5 for each stitch until you have the desired number of stitches. Try 20 if you are practicing for the first time.

Note: If you're wondering in which order the strands of yarn should fall, a good guideline is always to have the tail end of the yarn around your thumb.

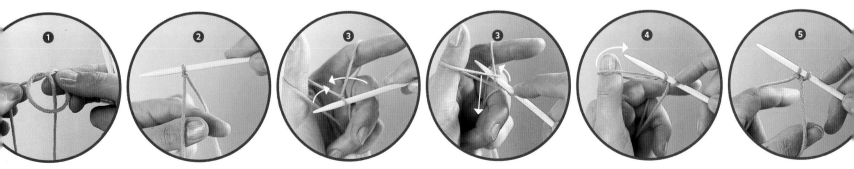

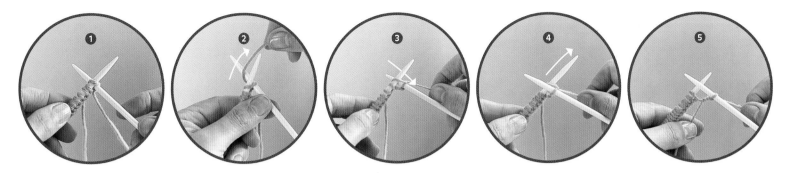

Knit Stitch

The basis of knitting is the knit stitch. Once you master it, anything is possible.

1. Place the needle with the stitches in your left hand. Slide the needle in your right hand into the first stitch, from left to right, under the left needle.

2. Wrap the yarn under the right needle, then over the top in a clockwise direction, holding it taut with your right hand.

3. Slide the right needle back, catching the stitch.

4. Slide the stitch off the left needle.

5. Now you have one knit stitch on the right needle.

Repeat steps 1–4 for each stitch.

When you have knit all the stitches on the needle, you have completed a row, and all the stitches are on the right needle. Place the needle back in your left hand and begin the steps again for another row.

Warning: The first stitch of each row is always a little loose but will tighten once you start knitting. The yarn should hang in front of the first stitch, so don't make the mistake of trying to swing it over to the back of the needle to "tighten" the stitch. This will make the first stitch look like 2 stitches, and your knitting will grow wider with every row.

If you continue to make rows of knit stitches, your knitting will look like the swatch at right on both sides. This is called Garter stitch, and you can make a scarf by casting on enough stitches for 5 or 6 inches (for more information on making a scarf, see the instructions for gauge on page 151).

Garter Stitch

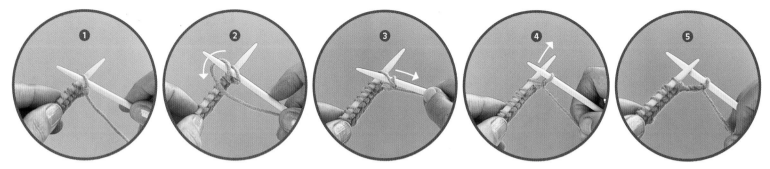

Purl Stitch

The purl stitch is very similar to the knit stitch. You just insert the needle and wrap the yarn in a different direction than you do when you make the knit stitch.

1. Place the needle with the stitches in your left hand. Slide the right needle into the first stitch, from right to left, on top of the left needle.

2. Wrap the yarn counterclockwise around the right needle.

3. Holding the yarn taut with your right hand, slide the needle back, catching the stitch under the left needle.

4. Slide the stitch off the left needle.

5. You now have a purl stitch on the right needle. Repeat steps 1–4 to continue.

Mel's Knitting Tips for Beginners

- Your yarn will always hang in front of the needle for the first stitch of the row.
- On a knit row, your yarn is at the back of the knitting.
- On a purl row, your yarn is in front of the knitting.
- In the middle of the row, your yarn is attached to the right needle. (This is helpful to know if you put your knitting down mid-row and wonder which direction you were going when you pick it up again.)
- There is a front and a back of a stitch. Always knit into the front of the stitch unless instructed otherwise.

If you work row after row of the purl stitch, your fabric will look the same as it would if you worked row after row of the knit stitch. In both cases, you are working Garter stitch. But once you have mastered the two stitches, you can start alternating knit and purl rows to create Stockinette stitch. Stockinette stitch is smooth on one side and bumpy on the other; the bumpy side is called Reverse Stockinette stitch.

Note: We don't recommend Stockinette stitch for a scarf as it rolls at the edges and your scarf will turn into a tube.

Stockinette Stitch / Reverse Stockinette Stitch

TRACEY: What if you're left-handed, Mel?

MEL: These are the options for lefties:

- Some left-handed knitters like to knit right-handed.

- If you're not comfortable knitting right-handed, just reverse all the instructions. The result will be the same.

For another resource for left-handed knitting, see page 163.

Binding Off

When you finish work on a piece of knitting, you need to remove all of the stitches from the needle in a certain way to keep all of your hard work from unraveling. This is called binding off.

1. Knit 2 stitches.

2. Holding the first stitch firmly on the right-hand needle, insert your left needle into the stitch from the left.

3. Slide the first stitch over the second stitch and off the needle. Knit 1 stitch.

4. Repeat steps 2–3 until there is 1 stitch left on the right needle. Break the yarn, pull the end of the yarn through this stitch to close it permanently.

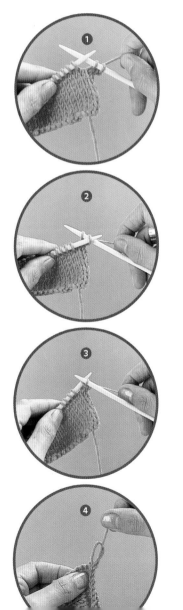

TRACEY: What else do I need to learn to shape a piece and follow a pattern?

MEL: Let's learn decreases, which will narrow our knitting.

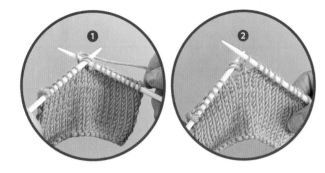

Decreasing by Knitting Two Stitches Together

K2tog makes a right-slanting decrease.

1. Slide the right needle into 2 stitches together as if to knit.

2. Complete the stitch as you would a normal knit stitch (in the photo for step 2, the 2 stitches knitted together are about to be dropped off the left needle; the stitch on the right needle is the one just created).

Decreasing with a Slip Slip Knit

Ssk makes a left-slanting decrease.

1. Insert the right needle into the first stitch as if to knit, and slide it onto the right needle. Slide a second stitch onto the right needle in the same way.

2. Insert the left needle into the two stitches on the right needle, from the left and on top of the right needle.

3. Wrap the yarn around the right needle as if to knit.

4. Catch the stitch and slide it off the left needle.

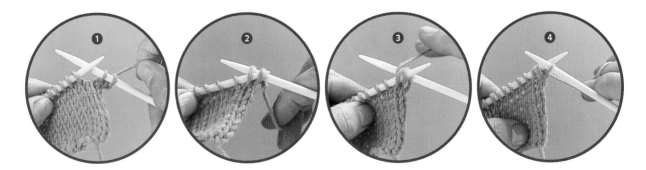

TRACEY: How do I make a piece wider?

MEL: By increasing. An easy way to do this is by knitting into the front and back of a stitch (kfb) to make two stitches.

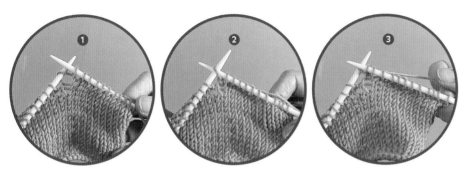

Increasing by Knitting into Front and Back of Stitch

Kfb makes two stitches out of one.

1. Knit the stitch you want to increase in but do not slide it off the left needle.

2. Take the needle around and knit into the back of the same stitch.

3. Slide the stitches off the left needle.

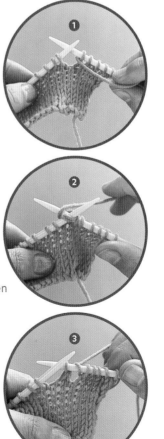

TRACEY: So, is this enough basic info to get started, Mel?

MEL: I think you'll need to know how to make a buttonhole, too. Here's an easy buttonhole that we use for our Baby Baseball Tee pattern on page 14.

Making a Buttonhole

1. Knit to the place where you wish to make a buttonhole. Take the yarn between the needles, around to the front of the knitting.

2. Knit the next 2 stitches together.

3. You will still have 2 stitches on the needle, since yarn in front of the needle will have created an extra stitch when followed by the k2tog.

Buttonhole

TRACEY: I've had a thought, Mel. Every beginner's nightmare is dropping a stitch. What do you do if this happens?

MEL: Practice by dropping a stitch off the needle on purpose. Now, stretch the knitting sideways to make it drop a few more rows. You'll see the dropped loop and stacked on top of it are several horizontal bars, which are the consecutive stitches that you must now pick up and draw through the dropped loop one by one. A crochet hook two sizes smaller than your knitting needles is handy for this purpose.

Picking Up Dropped Stitches on the Knit Side

1. Find the drooped loop and slide a crochet hook into the front of the stitch.

2. Catch the horizontal bar behind the stitch, pull it through the loop, and place it back on the left needle.

Picking Up Dropped Stitches on the Purl Side

1. Find the dropped loop and slide a crochet hook into it from the back.

   Catch the horizontal bar in front of the stitch.

2. Slide the bar through the loop.

3. Place it back on the left needle.

TRACEY: Getting to the end of a project can be a bit scary, Mel. You've waited so long for all the pieces of the puzzle to be complete. Now you think, what if I sew it all together, put it on, and don't look like the willowy model leaning against the barn door in the photo?

MEL: Take a deep breath, and don't rush this part. I know the feeling of chomping at the bit to finally wear something, but to finish a knitted garment well you need to stay calm. If you're bleary-eyed and it's one in the morning, imagine a stern voice telling you: "Step away from the yarn, step away. Put it down and go to sleep. It will still be there in the morning, and nobody will have got hurt. So, step away from the yarn, Ma'am."

Whipstitch and Mattress Stitch

Here are instructions for two stitches that can be used to sew together the different pieces of a project.

Whipstitch creates a flat seam that can be seen on the outside of the garment.

Whipstitch   **Mattress Stitch**

- Line the two knitted pieces up side by side, with the wrong side facing out.

- Take the threaded needle through the edge stitch on each side, left to right or right to left.

Mattress stitch creates a seam that is invisible on the outside but bulky on the inside.

- With the right (or public) sides of the two knitted pieces facing out, find the horizontal bar between the edge stitch and the next stitch on both pieces.

- Insert the threaded needle through these two bars, first the right bar, then the left. Pull to tighten the seam as you go.

TRACEY: Mel, how do you gain confidence and improve?

MEL: Get a book with lots of different stitches in it. Practice doing different stitches. Choose a pattern you really like that inspires you. On page 163 is a list of some of my favorite books.

TRACEY: Remember when I came to your shop, and I'd only knitted a few easy things, and you said to me, why don't you try this now?

MEL: And I showed you the Debbie Bliss blackberry stitch jacket.

TRACEY: I nearly fainted!

MEL: But I knew with your terrier-like tenacity you would figure it out.

TRACEY: I did, and it's still one of the best things I've made. What shall I knit next, Mel?

MEL: I heard about a woman in Australia who knitted a slipcover for her house.

TRACEY: Get outta here!

MEL: It's true.

TRACEY: (pause) Be very expensive in cashmere . . .

Sources for Supplies

If you cannot find the supplies called for in the patterns in this book at your local yarn shop, contact these wholesalers, who can direct you to the most convenient source.

Alchemy Yarns
Sebastopol, CA
707-823-3276
www.alchemyyarns.com

Artemis Exquisite Embellishments
(Hanah Silk Ribbon)
Eureka, CA
888-233-5187
www.artemisinc.com

Blue Sky Alpacas, Inc
St Francis, MN
763-753-5815
www.blueskyalpacas.com

Bryson Distributing
(knitting needles and accessories)
Eugene, OR
541-485-1884
www.brysonknits.com

Cascade Yarns
Tukwila, WA
206-574-0440
www.cascadeyarns.com

Classic Elite Yarns, Inc
Lowell, MA
978-453-2837
www.classiceliteyarns.com

Crystal Palace Yarns
Richmond, CA
510-237-9988
www.straw.com

Design Source (Manos del Uruguay)
Stoneham, MA
781-438-9631

Habu Textiles
New York, NY
212-239-3546
www.habutextiles.com

Karabella Yarns
New York, NY
212-684-2665
www.karabellayarns.com

Knitting Fever, Inc
(Euro Yarns/Linie and Noro Yarns)
Amityville, NY
516-546-3600
www.knittingfever.com

Koigu Wool Designs
Williamsford, ON Canada
519-794-3066
www.koigu.com

Louet Sales (Euroflax)
Ogdensburg, NY
613-925-4502
www.louet.com

Muench Yarns, Inc (GGH Yarns)
Petaluma, CA
707-763-9377
www.muenchyarns.com

Needful Yarns, Inc
(Lana Gatto, Filtes King)
Toronto, ON Canada
416-398-3700
www.needfulyarnsinc.com

Renaissance Buttons
Bayfield, CO
970-884-9620
www.renaissancebuttons.com

Renaissance Ribbons
Oregon House, CA
877-422-6601
www.renaissanceribbons.com

Rio de la Plata Yarns
Marina del Ray, CA
310-827-3535
www.riodelaplatayarns.com

Skacel Collection (knitting needles)
Seattle, WA
425-291-9600
www.skacelknitting.com

Sunbelt Fasteners
(purse handles, bamboo rods)
Culver City, CA
310-836-5212
www.sunbeltfashion.com

Tahki Stacy Charles (Filatura Di Crosa)
Ridgewood, NY
718-326-4433
www.tahkistacycharles.com

Unbuttons (vintage buttons)
707-942-2132
www.unbuttons.com

Westminster Fibers, Inc
(Rowan and Jaegar Yarns)
Nashua, NH
603-886-5041
www.knitrowan.com

Mel's Picks: Recommended Reading

I Taught Myself Knitting (Boye)

An inexpensive pamphlet with clear how-to drawings and a special section for left-handed knitters.

Vogue Knitting: The Ultimate Knitting Book by the Editors of *Vogue Knitting* (Sixth & Spring)

This book has information on stitches and techniques, as well as a section on pattern-making.

365 Knitting Stitches a Year Perpetual Calendar (Martingale)

A great resource for stitch patterns, in a handy size that fits easily into your handbag.

A Treasury of Knitting Patterns by Barbara Walker (Schoolhouse Press)

All four books in this series are valuable resources for learning new stitches.

The Knitter's Handy Book of Patterns by Ann Budd (Interweave Press)

I use this book regularly for making socks, gloves, and sweaters. It offers a template for using different gauges and varying sizes, making it easy to customize your patterns.

The Ultimate Sourcebook of Knitting and Crochet Stitches by the Editors of *Reader's Digest* (Reader's Digest)

Color photographs of stitches and excellent how-to instructions for knitting and crochet.

Mary Thomas's Knitting Book and **Mary Thomas's Book of Knitting Patterns** (Dover)

These books were originally published in the 1940s. They are full of fascinating information about the history of knitting and contain excellent instructions on knitting techniques, designing, and stitch patterns.

Knitting Essentials: Knitter's Historical Pattern Series / Volume One by Melissa Johnson (Pastime Publications)

A good resource for lace patterns.

Knitting: 19th-Century Sources edited by Jules and Kaethe Kliot (Lacis Publications)

A fascinating book filled with drawings and patterns for knitted items popular in the 19th century.

Special Techniques

Cable Cast-On
Make a loop (using a slipknot) with the working yarn and place it on the left-hand needle [first st cast on], knit into slip knot, draw up a loop but do not drop st from left hand needle; place new loop on left-hand needle; *insert the tip of the right-hand needle into the space between the last 2 sts on the left-hand needle and draw up a loop; place the loop on the left-hand needle. Repeat from * for remaining stitches to be cast on, or for casting on at the beginning of a row in progress.

Crochet Chain
Make a slipknot and place it on crochet hook. Holding tail end of yarn in left hand, *take hook under ball end of yarn from front to back; draw yarn on hook back through previous st on hook to form new st. Repeat from * to desired number of sts or length of chain.

Garter Stitch
Knit every row when working on straight needles; knit 1 round, purl 1 round when working in the round.

I-Cord
Using a double-pointed needle cast on or pick up the required number of sts; the working yarn will be at the left-hand side of the needle. * Transfer the needle with the sts to your left hand, bring the yarn around behind the work to the right-hand side; using a second double pointed needle, knit the stitches from right to left, pulling the yarn from left to right for the first st; do not turn. Slide the stitches to the opposite end of the needle; repeat from * until the cord is the length desired. *Note: After a few rows, the tubular shape will become apparent.*

Intarsia Colorwork Method
Use a separate length of yarn for each color section. When changing colors, bring the new yarn up and to the right of the yarn just used to twist the yarns and prevent leaving a hole; do not carry colors not in use across the back of the work.

Kitchener Stitch
Using a blunt yarn needle, thread a length of yarn approximately 4 times the length of the section to be joined. Hold the pieces to be joined wrong sides together, with the needles holding the stitches parallel, both ends pointing in the same direction. Working from right to left, insert yarn needle into first st on front needle as if to purl, pull yarn through, leaving st on needle; insert yarn into first st on back needle as if to knit, pull yarn through, leaving st on needle; *insert yarn needle in first stitch on front needle as if to knit, pull yarn through, remove st from needle; insert yarn needle into next st on front needle as if to purl, pull yarn through, leave st on needle; insert yarn needle

into first st on back needle as if to purl, pull yarn through, remove st from needle; insert yarn needle into next st on back needle as if to knit, pull yarn through, leave st on needle. Repeat from *, working 3 or 4 stitches at a time, then go back and adjust tension to match the pieces being joined. When 1 st remains on each needle, cut yarn and pass through last 2 sts to fasten off.

Knitted Cast-On
Make a loop (using a slip knot) with the working yarn and place it on the left-hand needle [first st cast on], *knit into the stitch on the left-hand needle, draw up a loop but do not drop st from left-hand needle; place new loop on left-hand needle; repeat from * for remaining stitches to be cast on, or for casting on at the beginning of a row in progress.

Pompom
You can use a pompom maker or the following method: Cut two cardboard circles in the diameter of the pompom desired. Cut a 1" diameter hole in the center of each circle. Cut away a small wedge out of each circle to allow for wrapping yarn. Hold the circles together with the openings aligned. Wrap yarn around the circles until there is no room left in the center to wrap. Carefully cut yarn around outer edge of the cardboard circles. Using a 12" length of yarn, wrap around strands between the two

circles and tie tightly. Slip the cardboard circles off the completed pompom; trim pompom, leaving the ends of the tie untrimmed. Using ends of tie, sew pompom to garment.

Reading Charts

Unless otherwise specified in the instructions, when working on straight needles, Charts are read from right to left for RS rows, from left to right for WS rows. Row numbers are written at the beginning of each row. Numbers on the right indicate RS rows; numbers on left indicate WS rows. When working in the round, all rounds are read from right to left.

Reverse Stockinette Stitch (Rev St st)

Purl on RS rows, knit on WS rows when working on straight needles; purl every round when working in the round.

Ribbing

Although rib stitch patterns use different numbers of stitches, all are worked in the same way, whether on straight needles or in the round. The instructions will specify how many sts to knit or purl; the example below uses k1, p1.

Row/Rnd 1: * K1, p1; repeat from * across, (end k1 if an odd number of stitches).

Row/Rnd 2: Knit the knit stitches and purl the purl stitches as they face you.

Repeat Row/Rnd 2 for rib st.

Seed Stitch

Row/Rnd 1:* K1, p1; repeat from * across, (end k1 if an odd number of sts).

Row Rnd 2: Knit the purls and purl the knits as they face you.

Repeat Row/Rnd 2 for Seed st.

Stockinette Stitch (St st)

Knit on RS rows, purl on WS rows when working on straight needles; knit every round when working in the round.

Stranded (Fair Isle) Colorwork Method

When more than one color is used per row, carry color(s) not in use loosely across the WS of work. Be sure to secure all colors at beginning and end of rows to prevent holes.

Tassel

Using color of your choice, wind yarn 20 times (or to desired thickness) around a piece of cardboard or other object the same length as desired for Tassel. Slide yarn needle threaded with matching yarn under the strands at the top of the tassel; tie tightly, leaving ends long enough for attaching Tassel to garment. Cut through all strands at the opposite end. Tie a second piece of yarn tightly around the Tassel several times, approximately $1/2$" from top of Tassel; secure ends inside top of Tassel. Trim ends even; attach to garment.

Three-Needle Bind-Off

Place the stitches to be joined onto two same-size needles; hold the pieces to be joined with the right or wrong sides facing each other, as indicated in the pattern, and the needles parallel, both pointing to the right. Holding both needles in your left hand, using working yarn and a third needle same size or one size larger, insert third needle into back of first stitch on front needle, then into front of first st on back needle; knit these two sts together; * knit next stitch from each needle together (two stitches on right-hand needle); pass first stitch over second stitch to bind off one stitch. Repeat from * until one stitch remains on third needle; cut yarn and fasten off.

Twisted Cord

Take a strand of yarn and secure one end to a stationary object. Twist from other end until it begins to buckle. Fold twisted length in half and holding ends together, allow to twist up on itself. Tie cut end in an overhand knot to secure.

Yarnover

Bring yarn forward (to the purl position), then place it in position to work the next st. If next st is to be knit, bring yarn over the needle and knit; if next st is to be purled, bring yarn over the needle and then forward again to the purl position and purl. Work the yarnover in pattern on the next row unless instructed otherwise.

Abbreviations

Circ Circular

Dpn Double-pointed needle(s)

K Knit

K2tog Knit 2 sts together.

K3tog Knit 3 sts together.

Kfb Knit into front loop and back loop of same stitch to increase one stitch.

Mb Make bobble (as instructed).

MC Main color

M1 (make 1-left slanting) With the tip of the left-hand needle inserted from front to back, lift the strand between the two needles onto the left-hand needle; knit the strand through the back loop to increase one stitch.

M1p (make 1 purlwise) With the tip of the left-hand needle inserted from back to front, lift the strand between the two needles onto the left-hand needle; purl the strand through the front loop to increase one stitch.

P Purl

P2tog Purl 2 sts together.

Pfb Purl the next st through the front of its loop, then through the back of its loop, to increase one st.

Pm Place marker

Psso (pass slipped stitch over) Pass slipped st on right-hand needle over the sts indicated in the instructions, as in binding off.

Rnd Round

RS Right side

Skp (slip, knit, pass) Slip next st knitwise to right-hand needle, k1, pass slipped st over knit st.

Sk2p (double decrease) Slip next st knitwise to right-hand needle, k2tog, pass slipped st over st from k2tog.

Sl (slip) Slip stitch(es) as if to purl, unless otherwise specified.

Sl st (crochet slip stitch) Insert hook in st, yarn over hook, and draw through loop on hook.

Sm Slip marker

Spp (slip, purl, pass) Slip next st knitwise to right-hand needle, p1, pass slipped st over purled st.

Sp2p (double decrease) Slip next st knitwise to right-hand needle, p2tog, pass slipped st over st from p2tog.

Ssk (slip, slip, knit) Slip the next 2 sts to the right-hand needle one at a time as if to knit; insert left-hand needle into 2 slipped sts from the left and on top of the right-hand needle, knit the 2 sts together.

St(s) stitch(es)

K1-tbl Knit one stitch through the back loop, twisting the stitch.

Tbl Through the back loop

Tog Together

WS Wrong side

Wyib With yarn in back

Wyif With yarn in front

Yb Yarn back

Yf Yarn front

Yo Yarnover

Acknowledgments

Tracey and Mel would like to thank:

Lori Lober, Anna Christian, Melanie Falick, Amy Ross, Shalini Waran, Asta Dargiene, Dale Hagen, Julie Dickover, Eliza Smith, Lisbeth Nilson, Irene Lober, Reggie and Alou Dechard, Angela Dechard, Maclaren and Stephanie Laing, Ivy and Tracy Wolk, Sally Sutton, Audree Futterman, Matt Kanji, Pepe Leon, Sophie Gnamien, Renee Pietrangelo, Liz Cullumber, John Millhauser, Sue McCain, Patricia Roberts, Jill and Jeff Harris, Paula and Jim Allen, Karen Kaplan, and the sheep Gracie and Albert (aka Fluffy and Maude).

Personal thanks from Mel:

Thank you to all the Wildfiber customers who support the store and enable me to continue to do something I love.

Tracey and Mel Cast Off

TRACEY: So, do you think we covered it all, Mel?

MEL: No, that would be impossible. But we made a start—and, hopefully, inspired a few people.

TRACEY: What words of wisdom can we leave our readers with?

MEL: Don't stop knitting, even in summer. Knitting is a good companion and will always be there for you.

TRACEY: And I would like to say quite simply—Go Home!! Go home! And knit.